D1194659

16 knitting designs in
Cashsoft Aran & Cashsoft
Chunky by Martin Storey

Escape to the wild Scottish Highlands
in Classic Travel, with a collection of
Aran and chunky weight knits for your
journey to cold and windswept
climates. Travel is its own pleasure so
enjoy your adventures in cape coats
and double breasted jackets, cardigans
and a long tunic that are influenced by
traditional fairisles and chunky cables.
Classic Travel features a new yarn,
Classic Cashsoft Chunky, a wonderful
addition to the hugely popular Cashsoft
range. The palette vibrates with the
colours and atmosphere of
the Highlands.
Bon Voyage!

the designs

Vintage delights. A walk in the hills, a stroll in the valleys.
Breathless laughter and the excitement of the journey.

18 **Munro**
[mens version] ★
Cashsoft Chunky
Pattern page 71

20 **Moffat** ▲
Cashsoft Aran
Pattern page 65

21 **Cameron**
[mens version] ★
Cashsoft Chunky
Pattern page 55

25 **Cameron**
[ladies version] ▲
Cashsoft Chunky
Pattern page 52

34 **Morgan** ▲
Cashsoft Chunky
Pattern page 67

36 **Douglas** ★
Cashsoft Aran
Pattern page 60

37 **Regan** ▲
Cashsoft Aran
Pattern page 76

40 **Georgia** ▲
Cashsoft Aran
Pattern page 63

SIZE KEY: ▲ Size S - XL   ★ Size S - XXL (Mens)   ✚ Accessory (Refer to pattern page)

designersnotebook

Brodie – Perfect for your journey, this cape-sleeved, crew neck jacket has a lovely fringe detail and tie belt. Pattern instructions page 50

The pleasure of travel, a winter odyssey

Angus sweater & hat – Both the Angus sweater and hat feature a bi-colour, ski-inspired fairisle. Pattern instructions pages 46 & 49

Christie – A double-breasted garter stitch coat with a scarf neck detail.
Pattern instructions page 58

Paisley coat & hat – A delightful beanie hat and long coat to keep you warm on your travels knitted in a traditional Shetland fairisle pattern. Pattern instructions page 72 & 75

Munro – Our wide rib stitch sweater for men has raglan sleeves and a soft roll collar. Pattern instructions page 71

Moffat – A delightful, traditional cable sweater with a moss stitch and rib collar. Pattern instructions page 65

Cameron [mens version] – This bowling cardigan is knitted in a vintage fairisle stitch. Pattern instructions page 55

Take to the air and see the landscape laid out like a beautiful patchwork. Free as a bird, you can choose where to go.

Cameron [ladies version]
For ladies, a cropped bowling
cardigan in a vintage fairisle stitch.
Pattern instructions page 52

Erin – This full-length gilet is simple to
knit in a ribbed stitch with fringed detail
at hem.
Pattern instructions page 62

Sydney – Keep warm in a little cardigan with a deep neck in a texture which creates a basket weave stitch.
Pattern instructions page 79

A deserted station, an early morning train,
another adventure around the corner.

Munro [ladies version] – A classic wide rib-stitch
sweater with flattering raglan sleeves and soft
roll collar. Pattern instructions page 70

Muir – This updated, poncho-style knit features a cable detail and deep ribbed cuffs
Pattern instructions page 68

Morgan – A pretty over-tunic with a deep neck opening in a garter stripe stitch pattern.
Pattern instructions page 67

Douglas – Men's double-breasted jacket with rib shawl collar in a rib and stag-horn cable stitch.
Pattern instructions page 60

Regan
A wonderfully feminine gilet with a cabled belt detail.
Pattern instructions page 76

Let me take you on a magical journey through a wild landscape. Making memories that are precious.

Georgia – An elegant sleeveless, cabled tunic with a deep, wrap-over shawl collar.
Pattern instructions page 63

Tension

Obtaining the correct tension is perhaps the single factor which can make the difference between a successful garment and a disastrous one. It controls both the shape and size of an article, so any variation, however slight, can distort the finished garment. Different designers feature in our books and it is **their** tension, given at the **start** of each pattern, which you must match. We recommend that you knit a square in pattern and/or stocking stitch (depending on the pattern instructions) of perhaps 5 - 10 more stitches and 5 - 10 more rows than those given in the tension note. Mark out the central 10cm square with pins. If you have too many stitches to 10cm try again using thicker needles, if you have too few stitches to 10cm try again using finer needles. Once you have achieved the correct tension your garment will be knitted to the measurements indicated in the size diagram shown at the end of the pattern.

Sizing and Size Diagram Note

The instructions are given for the smallest size. Where they vary, work the figures in brackets for the larger sizes. **One set of figures refers to all sizes.** Included with most patterns in this magazine is a **'size diagram'**, or sketch of the finished garment and its dimensions. The size diagram shows the finished width of the garment at the under-arm point, and it is this measurement that the knitter should choose first; a useful tip is to measure one of your own garments which is a comfortable fit. Having chosen a size based on width, look at the corresponding length for that size; if you are not happy with the total length which we recommend, adjust your own garment before beginning your armhole shaping - any adjustment after this point will mean that your sleeve will not fit into your garment easily - don't forget to take your adjustment into account if there is any side seam shaping. Finally, look at the sleeve length; the size diagram shows the finished sleeve measurement, taking into account any top-arm insertion length. Measure your body between the centre of your neck and your wrist, this measurement should correspond to half the garment width plus the sleeve length. Again, your sleeve length may be adjusted, but remember to take into consideration your sleeve increases if you do adjust the length - you must increase more frequently than the pattern states to shorten your sleeve, less frequently to lengthen it.

Chart Note

Many of the patterns in the book are worked from charts. Each square on a chart represents a stitch and each line of squares a row of knitting. Each colour used is given a different letter and these are shown in the **materials** section, or in the **key** alongside the chart of each pattern. When working from the charts, read odd rows (K) from right to left and even rows (P) from left to right, unless otherwise stated.

Knitting with colour

There are two main methods of working colour into a knitted fabric: Intarsia and Fairisle techniques. The first method produces a single thickness of fabric and is usually used where a colour is only required in a particular area of a row and does not form a repeating pattern across the row, as in the fairisle technique.

Intarsia: The simplest way to do this is to cut short lengths of yarn for each motif or block of colour used in a row. Then joining in the various colours at the appropriate point on the row, link one colour to the next by twisting them around each other where they meet on the wrong side to avoid gaps. All ends can then either be darned along the colour join lines, as each motif is completed or then can be "knitted-in" to the fabric of the knitting as each colour is worked into the pattern. This is done in much the same way as "weaving-in" yarns when working the Fairisle technique and does save time darning-in ends. It is essential that the tension is noted for Intarsia as this may vary from the stocking stitch if both are used in the same pattern.

Fairisle type knitting: When two or three colours are worked repeatedly across a row, strand the yarn not in use loosely behind the stitches being worked. If you are working with more than two colours, treat the "floating"yarns as if they were one yarn and always spread the stitches to their correct width to keep them elastic. It is advisable not to carry the stranded or "floating" yarns over more than three stitches at a time, but to weave them under and over the colour you are working. The "floating" yarns are caught at the back of the work.

Finishing Instructions

After working for hours knitting a garment, it seems a great pity that many garments are spoiled because such little care is taken in the pressing and finishing process. Follow the following tips for a truly professional-looking garment.

Pressing

Block out each piece of knitting and following the instructions on the ball band press the garment pieces, omitting the ribs. Tip: Take special care to press the edges, as this will make sewing up both easier and neater. If the ball band indicates that the fabric is not to be pressed, then covering the blocked out fabric with a damp white cotton cloth and leaving it to stand will have the desired effect. Darn in all ends neatly along the selvedge edge or a colour join, as appropriate.

Stitching

When stitching the pieces together, remember to match areas of colour and texture very carefully where they meet. Use a seam stitch such as back stitch or mattress stitch for all main knitting seams and join all ribs and neckband with mattress stitch, unless otherwise stated.

Construction

Having completed the pattern instructions, join left shoulder and neckband seams as detailed above. Sew the top of the sleeve to the body of the garment using the method detailed in the pattern, referring to the appropriate guide:

Set-in sleeves: Place centre of cast-off edge of sleeve to shoulder seam. Set in sleeve, easing sleeve head into armhole.

Straight cast-off sleeves: Place centre of cast-off edge of sleeve to shoulder seam. Sew top of sleeve to body.

Join side and sleeve seams.
Slip stitch pocket edgings and linings into place. Sew on buttons to correspond with buttonholes. Ribbed welts and neckbands and any area of garter stitch should not be pressed.

Abbreviations

K	knit	psso	pass slipped
P	purl		stitch over
st(s)	stitch(es)	tbl	through back
inc	increas(e)(ing)		of loop
dec	decreas(e)(ing)	M1	make one stitch
st st	stocking stitch		by picking up
	(1 row K, 1 row P)		horizontal loop
g st	garter stitch		before next stitch
	(K every row)		and working into
beg	begin(ning)		back of it
foll	following	yrn	yarn round needle
rem	remain(ing)	yfwd	yarn forward
rep	repeat	yon	yarn over needle
alt	alternate	yfrn	yarn forward and
cont	continue		round needle
patt	pattern	meas	measures
tog	together	o	no stitches,
mm	millimetres		times, or rows
cm	centimetres	-	no stitches, times
in(s)	inch(es)		or rows for that
RS	right side		size
WS	wrong side	approx	approximately
sl 1	slip one stitch	rev	reverse
sl 2	slip two stitches		

 = Easy, straight forward knitting/crocheting   = Suitable for the average knitter   = For the more experienced knitter

Main image page 14

 Angus

YARN

	S	M	L	XL	XXL	
To fit chest	102	107	112	117	122	cm
	40	42	44	46	48	in
Rowan RYC Cashsoft Aran						
A Kale 007	13	14	15	16	17	x 50gm
B Cream 013	4	5	5	5	6	x 50gm

NEEDLES

1 pair 4mm (no 8) (US 6) needles
1 pair 4½mm (no 7) (US 7) needles

TENSION

20 sts and 22 rows to 10 cm measured over

patterned stocking stitch using 4½mm (US 7) needles.

BACK

Using 4mm (US 6) needles and yarn A cast on 110 [114: 122: 126: 134] sts.
Row 1 (RS): K2, *P2, K2, rep from * to end.
Row 2: P2, *K2, P2, rep from * to end.
These 2 rows form rib.
Work in rib for a further 19 rows, ending with **WS** facing for next row.
Row 22 (WS): Rib 7 [5: 10: 7: 10], M1, (rib 16 [13: 17: 14: 19], M1) 6 [8: 6: 8: 6] times, rib to end. 117 [123: 129: 135: 141] sts.

Change to 4½mm (US 7) needles.
Beg and ending rows as indicated, using the **fairisle** technique as described on the information page, working chart rows 1 to 6 **once only** and then repeating chart rows 7 to 82 throughout, work from chart for body, which is worked entirely in st st beg with a K row, as folls:
Cont straight until back meas approx 43 [44: 43: 44: 43] cm, ending after chart row 78 [80: 78: 80: 78] and with RS facing for next row.
Shape armholes
Keeping patt correct, cast off 6 sts at beg of next 2 rows. 105 [111: 117: 123: 129] sts.
Dec 1 st at each end of next 5 [5: 5: 3: 3] rows,

Body

Key
A
B

then on foll 3 [2: 1: 2: 1] alt rows, then on foll 4th
row. 87 [95: 103: 111: 119] sts.
Cont straight until armhole meas 23 [24: 25:
26: 27] cm, ending with RS facing for next row.

Shape back neck and shoulders
Cast off 8 [10: 11: 12: 13] sts at beg of next 2 rows.
71 [75: 81: 87: 93] sts.
Next row (RS): Cast off 8 [10: 11: 12: 13] sts, patt
until there are 13 [13: 14: 16: 17] sts on right
needle and turn, leaving rem sts on a holder.
Work each side of neck separately.
Cast off 4 sts at beg of next row.
Cast off rem 9 [9: 10: 12: 13] sts.
With RS facing, rejoin yarns to rem sts, cast off
centre 29 [29: 31: 31: 33] sts, patt to end.
Complete to match first side, reversing shapings.

FRONT
Work as given for back until 14 [14: 16: 16: 18]
rows less have been worked than on back to beg
of shoulder shaping, ending with RS facing for
next row.

Shape neck
Next row (RS): Patt 32 [36: 40: 44: 48] sts and
turn, leaving rem sts on a holder.
Work each side of neck separately.
Keeping patt correct, dec 1 st at neck edge of next
4 rows, then on foll 2 [2: 3: 3: 4] alt rows, then on
foll 4th row. 25 [29: 32: 36: 39] sts.
Work 1 row, ending with RS facing for next row.

Shape back neck and shoulders
Cast off 8 [10: 11: 12: 13] sts at beg of next and
foll alt row.
Work 1 row.
Cast off rem 9 [9: 10: 12: 13] sts.
With RS facing, rejoin yarns to rem sts, cast off
centre 23 sts, patt to end.
Complete to match first side, reversing shapings.

SLEEVES
Using 4mm (US 6) needles and yarn A cast on
46 [50: 50: 54: 54] sts.
Work in rib as given for back for 21 rows, ending
with **WS** facing for next row.
Row 22 (WS): Rib 5 [8: 5: 9: 5], M1, (rib 9 [17: 10:
18: 11], M1) 4 [2: 4: 2: 4] times, rib to end.
51 [53: 55: 57: 59] sts.
Change to 4½mm (US 7) needles.

Sleeve

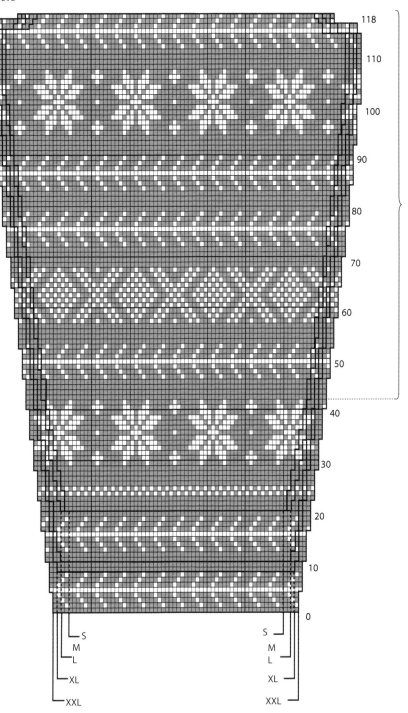

76 row patt repeat

Beg with a K row, work in st st for 2 [4: 0: 2: 0] rows, inc 0 [1: 0: 0: 0] st at each end of – [2nd: -: -: -] of these rows and ending with RS facing for next row. 51 [55: 55: 57: 59] sts.

Beg with chart row 21 [21: 11: 9: 1] and beg and ending rows as indicated, using the **fairisle** technique as described on the information page, working chart rows 21 [21: 11: 9: 1] to 118 **once only** and then repeating chart rows 43 to 118 as required, work from chart for sleeve, which is worked entirely in st st beg with a K row, as folls: Inc 1 st at each end of next [3rd: 3rd: 3rd: 5th] and every foll 4th [4th: 4th: 6th: 6th] row to 63 [61: 59: 87: 85] sts, then on every foll 6th [6th: 6th: 8th: 8th] row until there are 83 [85: 87: 89: 91] sts, taking inc sts into patt.

Cont straight until sleeve meas approx 53 [55: 57: 59: 61] cm, ending after chart row 114 [116: 114: 116: 114] and with RS facing for next row.

Shape top

Keeping patt correct, cast off 6 sts at beg of next 2 rows. 71 [73: 75: 77: 79] sts.

Dec 1 st at each end of next 5 rows, then on foll 3 alt rows. 55 [57: 59: 61: 63] sts.

Work 3 rows, ending with RS facing for next row.

Dec 1 st at each end of next and every foll alt row to 41 sts, then on foll 5 rows, ending with RS facing for next row. 31 sts.

Cast off 5 sts at beg of next 2 rows.

Cast off rem 21 sts.

MAKING UP

Press as described on the information page. Join right shoulder seam using back stitch, or mattress stitch if preferred.

Neckband

With RS facing, using 4mm (US 6) needles and yarn A, pick up and knit 17 [17: 20: 20: 21] sts down left side of neck, 23 sts from front, 17 [17: 20: 20: 21] sts up right side of neck, then 37 [37: 39: 39: 41] sts from back. 94 [94: 102: 102: 106] sts.

Beg with row 2, work in rib as given for back until neckband meas 9 cm from pick-up row, ending with RS facing for next row.

Cast off in rib.

See information page for finishing instructions, setting in sleeves using the set-in method.

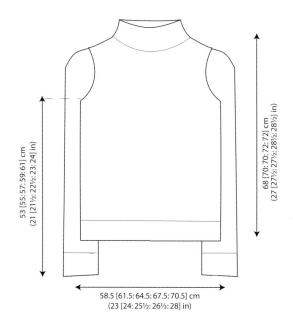

53 [55: 57: 59: 61] cm
(21 [21½: 22½: 23: 24] in)

68 [70: 70: 72: 72] cm
(27 [27½: 27½: 28½: 28½] in)

58.5 [61.5: 64.5: 67.5: 70.5] cm
(23 [24: 25½: 26½: 28] in)

Main image page 14

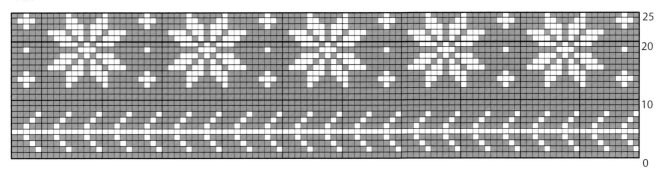

Angus hat

YARN

Rowan RYC Cashsoft Aran

A	Kale	007	2	x 50gm
B	Cream	013	1	x 50gm

NEEDLES

1 pair 4mm (no 8) (US 6) needles
1 pair 4½mm (no 7) (US 7) needles

TENSION

20 sts and 22 rows to 10 cm measured over patterned stocking stitch using 4½mm (US 7) needles.

HAT

Using 4mm (US 6) needles and yarn A, cast on 98 sts.

Row 1 (RS): K2, *P2, K2, rep from * to end.
Row 2: P2, *K2, P2, rep from * to end.
These 2 rows form rib.
Work in rib for a further 3 rows, ending with **WS** facing for next row.
Row 6 (WS): Rib 7, M1, (rib 14, M1) 6 times, rib 7. 105 sts.
Change to 4½mm (US 7) needles.
Beg and ending rows as indicated and using the **fairisle** technique as described on the information page, cont in patt from chart, which is worked entirely in st st beg with a K row, until all 25 rows of chart have been completed, ending with **WS** facing for next row.
Break off yarn B and cont using yarn A **only**.
Next row (WS): P6, P2tog, (P16, P2tog) 5 times, P7. 99 sts.

Shape crown

Row 1 (RS): (K5, K2tog) 14 times, K1. 85 sts.
Row 2 and every foll alt row: Purl.
Row 3: Knit.
Row 5: (K4, K2tog) 14 times, K1. 71 sts.
Row 7: Knit.
Row 9: (K3, K2tog) 14 times, K1. 57 sts.
Row 11: Knit.
Row 13: (K2, K2tog) 14 times, K1. 43 sts.
Row 15: (K1, K2tog) 14 times, K1. 29 sts.
Row 16: P1, (P2tog) 14 times.
Break yarn and thread through rem 15 sts. Pull up tight and fasten off securely.

MAKING UP

Press as described on the information page.
Join back seam.

Hat

Key

■ A
□ B

Main image page 10

Brodie

YARN

	S	M	L	XL
To fit bust	81-86	91-97	102-107	112-117 cm
	32-34	36-38	40-42	44-46 in

Rowan RYC Cashsoft Aran

	17	19	21	23	x 50gm

(photographed in Mole 003)

NEEDLES
1 pair 4mm (no 8) (US 6) needles
1 pair 4½mm (no 7) (US 7) needles

BUTTONS – 8 x 00410

TENSION
19 sts and 25 rows to 10 cm measured over stocking stitch using 4½mm (US 7) needles.

BACK
Using 4mm (US 6) needles cast on 98 [108: 118: 130] sts.
Work in g st for 8 rows, ending with RS facing for next row.
Change to 4½mm (US 7) needles.
Next row (RS): Knit.
Next row: K5, P to last 5 sts, K5.
Rep last 2 rows 14 times more, ending with RS facing for next row.
Beg with a K row, work in st st for 2 [4: 6: 8] rows, ending with RS facing for next row.
Next row (dec) (RS): K9, sl 1, K1, psso, K8, sl 1, K1, psso, K to last 21 sts, K2tog, K8, K2tog, K9.
Work 7 rows.
Rep last 8 rows once more, then rep first of these rows (the dec row) again. 86 [96: 106: 118] sts.
Work 9 rows, then rep the dec row again.
Rep last 10 rows once more. 78 [88: 98: 110] sts.
Cont straight until back meas 33 [34: 35: 36] cm, ending with RS facing for next row.
Shape for cape sleeves
Cast on 5 sts at beg of next 8 rows, then 4 sts at beg of foll 6 rows, then 3 sts at beg of next 6 rows. 160 [170: 180: 192] sts.
Inc 1 st at each end of next 5 rows, then on foll 6 alt rows, then on 7 [8: 9: 10] foll 4th rows, then on 3 foll 6th rows. 202 [214: 226: 240] sts.

Work 9 rows, ending with RS facing for next row.
Shape back neck
Next row (RS): K87 [93: 98: 105] and turn, leaving rem sts on a holder.
Work each side of neck separately.
Dec 1 st at beg of next row.
Shape shoulder and overarm seam
Cast off rem 86 [92: 97: 104] sts.
With RS facing, rejoin yarn to rem sts, cast off centre 28 [28: 30: 30] sts, K to end.
Complete to match first side, reversing shapings.

LEFT FRONT
Using 4mm (US 6) needles cast on 49 [54: 59: 65] sts.
Work in g st for 8 rows, ending with RS facing for next row.
Change to 4½mm (US 7) needles.
Next row (RS): Knit.
Next row: P to last 5 sts, K5.
Rep last 2 rows 14 times more, ending with RS facing for next row.
Beg with a K row, work in st st for 2 [4: 6: 8] rows, ending with RS facing for next row.
Next row (dec) (RS): K9, sl 1, K1, psso, K8, sl 1, K1, psso, K to end.
Work 7 rows.
Rep last 8 rows once more, then rep first of these rows (the dec row) again. 43 [48: 53: 59] sts.
Work 9 rows, then rep the dec row again.
Rep last 10 rows once more. 39 [44: 49: 55] sts.
Cont straight until left front meas 33 [34: 35: 36] cm, ending with RS facing for next row.
Shape for cape sleeves
Cast on 5 sts at beg of next and foll 3 alt rows, then 4 sts at beg of foll 3 alt rows, then 3 sts at beg of next 3 alt rows. 80 [85: 90: 96] sts.
Work 1 row, ending with RS facing for next row.
Inc 1 st at beg of next row and at same edge of foll 4 rows, then on foll 6 alt rows, then on 7 [8: 9: 10] foll 4th rows, then on foll 6th row. 99 [105: 111: 118] sts.
Work 4 [4: 2: 2] rows, ending with **WS** facing for next row.
Shape neck
Cast off 8 sts at beg of next row.

91 [97: 103: 110] sts.
Dec 1 st at neck edge of next 3 rows, then on foll 3 [3: 4: 4] alt rows, then on foll 4th row **and at same time** inc 1 st at cape edge of next [next: 3rd: 3rd] and foll 6th row. 86 [92: 97: 104] sts.
Work 5 rows, ending with RS facing for next row.
Shape shoulder and overarm seam
Cast off.

RIGHT FRONT
Using 4mm (US 6) needles cast on 49 [54: 59: 65] sts.
Work in g st for 8 rows, ending with RS facing for next row.
Change to 4½mm (US 7) needles.
Next row (RS): Knit.
Next row: K5, P to end.
Rep last 2 rows 14 times more, ending with RS facing for next row.
Beg with a K row, work in st st for 2 [4: 6: 8] rows, ending with RS facing for next row.
Next row (dec) (RS): K to last 21 sts, K2tog, K8, K2tog, K9.
Complete to match left front, reversing shapings.

MAKING UP
Press as described on the information page.
Join both shoulder and overarm seams using back stitch, or mattress stitch if preferred.
Neckband
With RS facing and using 4mm (US 6) needles, beg and ending at front opening edges, pick up and knit 26 [26: 28: 28] sts up right side of neck, 30 [30: 32: 32] sts from back, then 26 [26: 28: 28] sts down left side of neck. 82 [82: 88: 88] sts.
Work in g st for 6 rows, ending with **WS** facing for next row.
Cast off knitwise (on **WS**).
Button band
Using 4mm (US 6) needles cast on 8 sts.
Work in g st until this band, when slightly stretched, fits up entire left front opening edge, from cast-on edge to top of neckband, ending with **WS** facing for next row.
Cast off knitwise (on **WS**).
Slip stitch band in place.

Mark positions for 8 buttons on this band – first to come level with first dec row, last to come 1.5 cm below top of neckband, and rem 6 buttons evenly spaced between.

Buttonhole band

Work to match button band, with the addition of 8 buttonholes to correspond with positions marked for buttons on button band as folls:

Buttonhole row (RS): K3, cast off 2 sts (to make a buttonhole – cast on 2 sts over these cast-off sts on next row), K3.

Slip stitch band in place.

Cape sleeve borders (both alike)

Using 4mm (US 6) needles cast on 5 sts.

Work in g st until border, when slightly stretched, fits around entire cape sleeve edge, beg and ending at inner edge of first set of cast-on sts, ending with **WS** facing for next row.

Cast off knitwise (on **WS**).

Slip stitch band in place.

See information page for finishing instructions.

Belt

Using 4mm (US 6) needles cast on 8 sts.

Work in g st until belt meas 132 [142: 152: 162] cm, ending with **WS** facing for next row.

Cast off knitwise (on **WS**).

Cut 20 cm lengths of yarn and, using photograph as a guide, knot groups of 3 of these lengths through edge of cape sleeve border to form fringe.

71 [73: 76: 78] cm
(28 [28½: 30: 30½] in)

51.5 [57: 62: 68.5] cm
(20½ [22½: 24½: 27] in)

106.5 [112.5: 119: 126.5] cm
(42 [44½: 47: 50] in)

Main image page 24

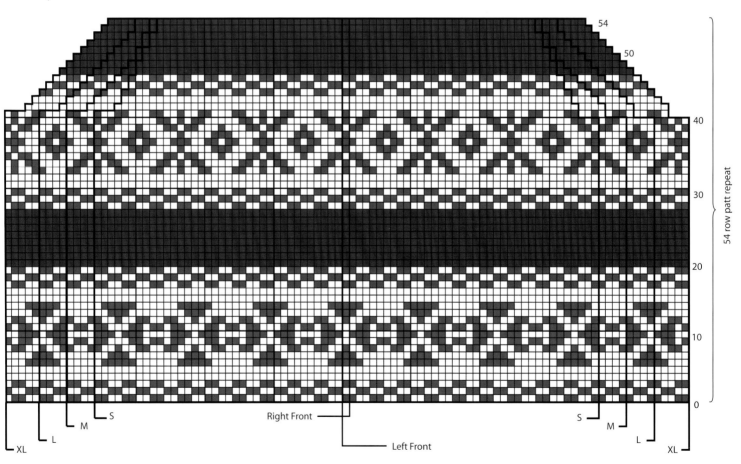

Cameron [ladies version]

YARN

	S	M	L	XL	
To fit bust	81-86	91-97	102-107	112-117	cm
	32-34	36-38	40-42	44-46	in

Rowan RYC Cashsoft Chunky

		S	M	L	XL	
A	Shiraz	711	8	9	10	11	x 50gm
B	Chalk	702	8	9	10	11	x 50gm
C	Skipper	707	3	3	3	4	x 50gm
D	Spinach	710	3	3	3	3	x 50gm

NEEDLES

1 pair 5mm (no 6) (US 8) needles
1 pair 6mm (no 4) (US 10) needles

BUTTONS – 5 x 00410

TENSION

15 sts and 20 rows to 10 cm measured over stocking stitch using 6mm (US 10) needles.

BACK

Using 5mm (US 8) needles and yarn A cast on 73 [81: 89: 99] sts.
Row 1 (RS): P0 [0: 1: 0], K2 [0: 3: 3], *P3, K3, rep from * to last 5 [3: 1: 0] sts, P3 [3: 1: 0], K2 [0: 0: 0].
Row 2: K0 [0: 1: 0], P2 [0: 3: 3], *K3, P3, rep from * to last 5 [3: 1: 0] sts, K3 [3: 1: 0], P2 [0: 0: 0].
These 2 rows form rib.
Work in rib for a further 14 rows, ending with RS facing for next row.

Change to 6mm (US 10) needles.
Beg with a K row, work in st st for 4 [6: 8: 10] rows, ending with RS facing for next row.
Beg and ending rows as indicated, using the **fairisle** technique as described on the information page and repeating the 54 row patt rep as required, cont in patt from chart for body, which is worked entirely in st st beg with a K row, as folls:
Cont straight until chart row 40 has been worked, ending with RS facing for next row.
Shape raglan armholes
Keeping patt correct, cast off 3 sts at beg of next 2 rows. 67 [75: 83: 93] sts.
Dec 1 st at each end of next 1 [7: 11: 19] rows, then

Body

54 row patt repeat

54
50
40
30
20
10
0

S
M
L
XL
Right Front
Left Front
S
M
L
XL

on every foll alt row until 23 [23: 25: 25] sts rem.
Work 1 row, ending with RS facing for next row.
Cast off.

LEFT FRONT
Using 5mm (US 8) needles and yarn A cast on
37 [41: 45: 50] sts.
Row 1 (RS): Po [0: 1: o], K2 [0: 3: 3], *P3, K3, rep
from * to last 5 sts, P3, K2.
Row 2: P2, *K3, P3, rep from * to last 5 [3: 1: o] sts,
K3 [3: 1: o], P2 [0: 0: o].
These 2 rows form rib.
Work in rib for a further 14 rows, ending with RS
facing for next row.
Change to 6mm (US 10) needles.
Beg with a K row, work in st st for 4 [6: 8: 10] rows,
ending with RS facing for next row.
Beg and ending rows as indicated, cont in patt
from chart for body as folls:
Cont straight until chart row 40 has been worked,
ending with RS facing for next row.
Shape raglan armhole
Keeping patt correct, cast off 3 sts at beg of next
row. 34 [38: 42: 47] sts.
Work 1 row.
Dec 1 st at raglan armhole edge of next 1 [7: 11: 19]
rows, then on every foll alt row until 19 [19:
21: 21] sts rem, ending with **WS** facing for next row.
Shape neck
Keeping patt correct, cast off 5 sts at beg of next
row. 14 [14: 16: 16] sts.
Dec 1 st at neck edge of next 5 rows, then on foll
2 [2: 3: 3] alt rows **and at same time** dec 1 st at
raglan armhole edge of next and every foll alt
row. 2 sts.
Work 1 row, ending with RS facing for next row.
Next row: K2tog and fasten off.

RIGHT FRONT
Using 5mm (US 8) needles and yarn A cast on
37 [41: 45: 50] sts.
Row 1 (RS): K2, *P3, K3, rep from * to last 5 [3:
1: o] sts, P3 [3: 1: o], K2 [0: 0: o].
Row 2: Ko [0: 1: o], P2 [0: 3: o], *K3, P3, rep from
* to last 5 sts, K3, P2.
These 2 rows form rib.
Complete to match left front, reversing shapings.

SLEEVES
Using 5mm (US 8) needles and yarn A cast on
37 [39: 41: 41] sts.
Row 1 (RS): Po [0: 1: 1], K2 [3: 3: 3], *P3, K3, rep
from * to last 5 [0: 1: 1] sts, P3 [0: 1: 1], K2 [0: 0: o].
Row 2: Ko [0: 1: 1], P2 [3: 3: 3], *K3, P3, rep from *
to last 5 [0: 1: 1] sts, K3 [0: 1: 1], P2 [0: 0: o].
These 2 rows form rib.
Work in rib for a further 14 rows, ending with RS
facing for next row.
Change to 6mm (US 10) needles.

Beg with a K row, work in st st for 6 [8: 10: 10] rows,
inc 1 st at each end of 5th of these rows and
ending with RS facing for next row.
39 [41: 43: 43] sts.
Beg and ending rows as indicated, using the
fairisle technique as described on the
information page and repeating the 54 row patt
rep as required, cont in patt from chart for sleeve,
which is worked entirely in st st beg with a K row,
as folls:
Inc 1 st at each end of 5th [3rd: next: next] and

Sleeve

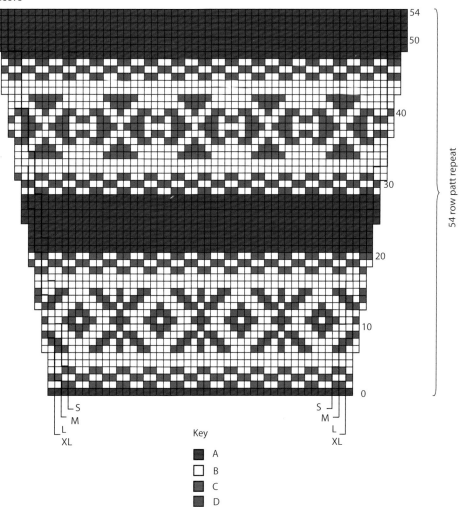

Key

■	A
□	B
■	C
■	D

every foll 6th row to 53 [53: 53: 61] sts, then on every foll 8th row until there are 57 [59: 61: 63] sts, taking inc sts into patt.

Cont straight until chart row 14 has been completed for the second time, ending with RS facing for next row.

Shape raglan

Keeping patt correct, cast off 3 sts at beg of next 2 rows. 51 [53: 55: 57] sts.

Dec 1 st at each end of next and every foll alt row until 11 sts rem.

Work 1 row, ending with RS facing for next row.

Left sleeve only

Dec 1 st at each end of next row, then cast off 2 sts at beg of foll row. 7 sts.

Dec 1 st at beg of next row, then cast off 3 sts at beg of foll row.

Right sleeve only

Cast off 3 sts at beg and dec 1 st at end of next row. 7 sts.

Work 1 row.

Rep last 2 rows once more.

Both sleeves

Cast off rem 3 sts.

MAKING UP

Press as described on the information page.

Join all raglan seams using back stitch, or mattress stitch if preferred.

Left front band and collar

Using 5mm (US 8) needles and yarn A cast on 6 sts. Work in g st until band, when slightly stretched, fits up left front opening edge, from cast-on edge

to neck shaping, ending with RS facing for next row.

Shape for collar

Inc 1 st at beg of next and every foll alt row until there are 28 sts.

Cont straight until collar section, unstretched, fits up left side of neck, across top of sleeve and across to centre back neck, ending with RS facing for next row.

Cast off.

Slip st band in place. Mark positions for 5 buttons

on this band – first to come 1 cm up from cast-on edge, last to come 1 cm below neck shaping, and rem 3 buttons evenly spaced between.

Right front band and collar

Work to match left front band and collar, reversing shapings and making 5 buttonholes to correspond with positions marked for buttons as folls:

Buttonhole row (RS): K2, K2tog, yfwd, K2.

Join cast-off ends of collar sections, then slip stitch bands and collar in place.

See information page for finishing instructions.

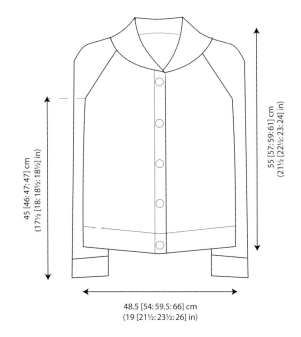

45 [46: 47: 47] cm (17½ [18: 18½: 18½] in)

55 [57: 59: 61] cm (21½ [22½: 23: 24] in)

48.5 [54: 59.5: 66] cm (19 [21½: 23½: 26] in)

Main image page 21

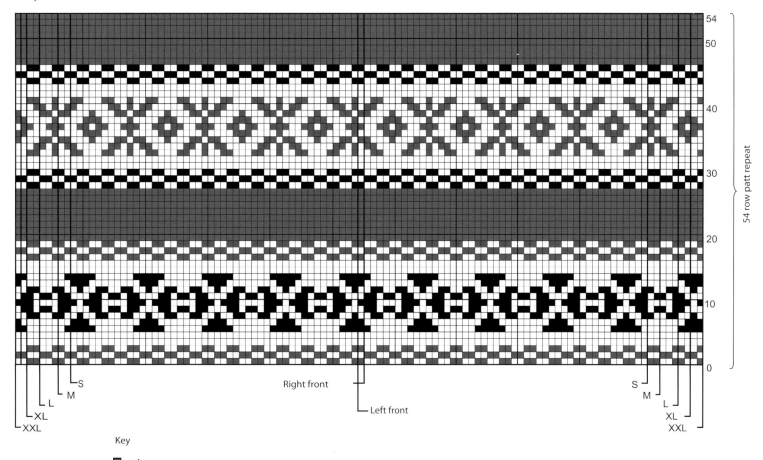

Cameron [mens version]

YARN

	S	M	L	XL	XXL	
To fit chest	102	107	112	117	122	cm
	40	42	44	46	48	in

Rowan RYC Cashsoft Chunky

A Skipper	707	11	12	13	14	15	x 50gm
B Chalk	702	11	11	12	13	13	x 50gm
C Black	712	4	4	4	5	5	x 50gm
D Spinach	710	3	3	4	4	4	x 50gm

NEEDLES

1 pair 5mm (no 6) (US 8) needles
1 pair 6mm (no 4) (US 10) needles

BUTTONS – 6 x 00339

TENSION

15 sts and 20 rows to 10 cm measured over stocking stitch using 6mm (US 10) needles.

BACK

Using 5mm (US 8) needles and yarn A cast on 93 [97: 103: 107: 111] sts.
Row 1 (RS): Po [0: 2: 0: 0], Ko [2: 3: 1: 3], *P3, K3, rep from * to last 3 [5: 2: 4: 0] sts, P3 [3: 2: 3: 0], Ko [2: 0: 1: 0].
Row 2: Ko [0: 2: 0: 0], Po [2: 3: 1: 3], *K3, P3, rep from * to last 3 [5: 2: 4: 0] sts, K3 [3: 2: 3: 0], Po [2: 0: 1: 0].
These 2 rows form rib.
Work in rib for a further 14 rows, ending with RS facing for next row.
Change to 6mm (US 10) needles.
Beg with a K row, work in st st for 4 [4: 4: 0: 0] rows, ending with RS facing for next row.
Beg and ending rows as indicated, using the **fairisle** technique as described on the information page and repeating the 54 row patt rep as required, cont in patt from chart for body, which is worked entirely in st st beg with a K row, as folls:

Key

- ▨ A
- ☐ B
- ■ C
- ▩ D

Work 58 [60: 58: 64: 62] rows, ending after chart
row 4 [6: 4: 10: 8] and with RS facing for next row.
Shape raglan armholes
Keeping patt correct, cast off 5 sts at beg of next
2 rows. 83 [87: 93: 97: 101] sts.
Dec 1 st at each end of next 7 [9: 11: 13: 13] rows,
then on every foll alt row until 23 [23: 25:
25: 27] sts rem.
Work 1 row, ending with RS facing for next row.
Cast off.

LEFT FRONT
Using 5mm (US 8) needles and yarn A cast on
47 [49: 52: 54: 56] sts.
Row 1 (RS): Po [0: 2: 0: 0], Ko [2: 3: 1: 3], *P3, K3,
rep from * to last 5 sts, P3, K2.
Row 2: P2, *K3, P3, rep from * to last 3 [5: 2:
4: 0] sts, K3 [3: 2: 3: 0], Po [2: 0: 1: 0].
These 2 rows form rib.
Work in rib for a further 14 rows, ending with RS
facing for next row.
Change to 6mm (US 10) needles.
Beg with a K row, work in st st for 4 [4: 4: 0: 0]
rows, ending with RS facing for next row.
Beg and ending rows as indicated, cont in patt
from chart for body as folls:
Work 58 [60: 58: 64: 62] rows, ending after chart
row 4 [6: 4: 10: 8] and with RS facing for next row.
Shape raglan armhole
Keeping patt correct, cast off 5 sts at beg of next
row. 42 [44: 47: 49: 51] sts.
Work 1 row.
Dec 1 st at raglan armhole edge of next 7 [9: 11:
13: 13] rows, then on every foll alt row until 19 [19:
21: 21: 23] sts rem, ending with **WS** facing for
next row.
Shape neck
Keeping patt correct, cast off 5 sts at beg of next
row. 14 [14: 16: 16: 18] sts.
Dec 1 st at neck edge of next 5 rows, then on foll
2 [2: 3: 3: 4] alt rows **and at same time** dec 1 st at
raglan armhole edge of next and every foll alt
row. 2 sts.
Work 1 row, ending with RS facing for next row.
Next row: K2tog and fasten off.

RIGHT FRONT
Using 5mm (US 8) needles and yarn A cast on

47 [49: 52: 54: 56] sts.
Row 1 (RS): K2, *P3, K3, rep from * to last 3 [5: 2:
4: 0] sts, P3 [3: 2: 3: 0], Ko [2: 0: 1: 0].
Row 2: Ko [0: 2: 0: 0], Po [2: 3: 1: 3], *K3, P3, rep
from * to last 5 sts, K3, P2.
These 2 rows form rib.
Complete to match left front, reversing shapings.

SLEEVES
Using 5mm (US 8) needles and yarn A cast on
43 [45: 47: 49: 51] sts.
Row 1 (RS): P2 [0: 0: 0: 0], K3 [0: 1: 2: 3], *P3, K3,
rep from * to last 2 [3: 4: 5: 0] sts, P2 [3: 3: 3: 0],
Ko [0: 1: 2: 0].
Row 2: K2 [0: 0: 0: 0], P3 [0: 1: 2: 3], *K3, P3, rep
from * to last 2 [3: 4: 5: 0] sts, K2 [3: 3: 3: 0],
Po [0: 1: 2: 0].
These 2 rows form rib.

Work in rib for a further 14 rows, ending with RS
facing for next row.
Change to 6mm (US 10) needles.
Beg with a K row, work in st st for 2 [4: 10: 8: 14]
rows, inc 1 st at each end of 0 [3rd: 3rd: 5th: 5th]
and foll 0 [0: 4th: 0: 6th] row and ending with RS
facing for next row. 43 [47: 51: 51: 55] sts.
Beg and ending rows as indicated, using the
fairisle technique as described on the
information page and repeating the 54 row patt
rep as required, cont in patt from chart for sleeve,
which is worked entirely in st st beg with a K row,
as folls:
Inc 1 st at each end of next [3rd: 3rd: 3rd: 3rd]
and every foll 4th [4th: 6th: 6th: 6th] row to
55 [53: 77: 79: 77] sts, then on every foll 6th [6th:
-: -: 8th] row until there are 73 [75: -: -: 81] sts,
taking inc sts into patt.

Sleeve

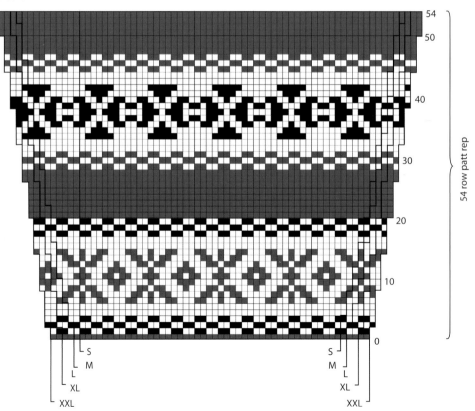

54 row patt rep

Cont straight until chart row 32 [34: 32: 38: 36] has been completed for the second time, ending with RS facing for next row.

Shape raglan

Keeping patt correct, cast off 5 sts at beg of next 2 rows. 63 [65: 67: 69: 71] sts.
Dec 1 st at each end of next 7 rows, then on every foll alt row until 7 sts rem.
Work 1 row, ending with RS facing for next row.

Left sleeve only

Place marker at beg of last row to denote top of front raglan seam.

Right sleeve only

Place marker at end of last row to denote top of front raglan seam.

Both sleeves

Dec 1 st at marked front edge of next 4 rows and at same time dec 1 st at back raglan edge of next and foll alt row, ending with RS facing for next row. 1 st.
Fasten off.

MAKING UP

Press as described on the information page.
Join all raglan seams using back stitch, or mattress stitch if preferred.

Right front band and collar

Using 5mm (US 8) needles and yarn A cast on 6 sts.
Work in g st until band, when slightly stretched, fits up right front opening edge, from cast-on edge to neck shaping, ending with RS facing for next row.

Shape for collar

Inc 1 st at end of next and every foll alt row until there are 28 sts.
Cont straight until collar section, unstretched, fits up right side of neck, across top of sleeve and across to centre back neck, ending with RS facing for next row.
Cast off.
Slip st band in place. Mark positions for 6 buttons on this band – first to come 1 cm up from cast-on edge, last to come 1 cm below neck shaping, and rem 4 buttons evenly spaced between.

Left front band and collar

Work to match right front band and collar, reversing shapings and making 6 buttonholes to correspond with positions marked for buttons as folls:

Buttonhole row (RS): K2, yfwd, K2tog, K2.
Join cast-off ends of collar sections, then slip stitch bands and collar in place.
See information page for finishing instructions.

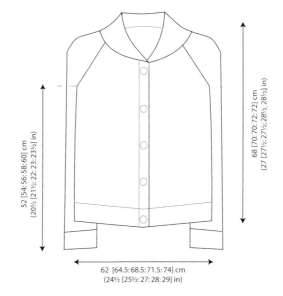

52 [54: 56: 58: 60] cm
(20½ [21½: 22: 23: 23½] in)

68 [70: 70: 72: 72] cm
(27 [27½: 27½: 28½: 28½] in)

62 [64.5: 68.5: 71.5: 74] cm
(24½ [25½: 27: 28: 29] in)

Main image page 15

 Christie

YARN

	S	M	L	XL
To fit bust	81-86	91-97	102-107	112-117 cm
	32-34	36-38	40-42	44-46 in

Rowan RYC Cashsoft Chunky

	28	31	34	37	x 50gm

(photographed in Spinach 710)

NEEDLES
1 pair 6mm (no 4) (US 10) needles

BUTTONS – 8 x 00345

TENSION
14 sts and 28 rows to 10 cm measured over garter stitch using 6mm (US 10) needles.

BACK
Using 6mm (US 10) needles cast on 91 [99: 107: 115] sts.
Work in g st, dec 1 st at each end of 11th and every foll 10th row to 71 [79: 87: 95] sts, then on every foll 12th row until 67 [75: 83: 91] sts rem.
Cont straight until back meas 49 [50: 51: 52] cm, ending with RS facing for next row.
Shape armholes
Cast off 5 sts at beg of next 2 rows.
57 [65: 73: 81] sts.
Dec 1 st at each end of next 3 [5: 5: 7] rows, then on foll 1 [2: 3: 3] alt rows, then on foll 4th row.
47 [49: 55: 59] sts.
Cont straight until armhole meas 22 [23: 24: 25] cm, ending with RS facing for next row.
Shape shoulders and back neck
Cast off 4 [4: 5: 6] sts at beg of next 2 rows.
39 [41: 45: 47] sts.
Next row (RS): Cast off 4 [4: 5: 6] sts, K until there are 8 [9: 9: 9] sts on right needle and turn, leaving rem sts on a holder.
Work each side of neck separately.

Cast off 4 sts at beg of next row.
Cast off rem 4 [5: 5: 5] sts.
With RS facing, rejoin yarn to rem sts, cast off centre 15 [15: 17: 17] sts, K to end.
Complete to match first side, reversing shapings.

LEFT FRONT
Using 6mm (US 10) needles cast on 57 [61: 65: 69] sts.
Work in g st, dec 1 st at beg of 11th and every foll 10th row to 47 [51: 55: 59] sts, then on every foll 12th row until 45 [49: 53: 57] sts rem.
Cont straight until left front matches back to beg of armhole shaping, ending with RS facing for next row.
Shape armhole
Cast off 5 sts at beg of next row. 40 [44: 48: 52] sts.
Work 1 row.
Dec 1 st at armhole edge of next 3 [5: 5: 7] rows, then on foll 1 [2: 3: 3] alt rows, then on foll 4th row. 35 [36: 39: 41] sts.
Cont straight until 17 [17: 19: 19] rows less have been worked than on back to beg of shoulder shaping, ending with **WS** facing for next row.
Shape neck
Cast off 16 sts at beg of next row.
19 [20: 23: 25] sts.
Dec 1 st at neck edge of next 3 rows, then on foll 2 [2: 3: 3] alt rows, then on 2 foll 4th rows.
12 [13: 15: 17] sts.
Work 1 row, ending with RS facing for next row.
Shape shoulder
Cast off 4 [4: 5: 6] sts at beg of next and foll alt row.
Work 1 row.
Cast off rem 4 [5: 5: 5] sts.
Mark positions for 4 pairs of buttons along left front opening edge – first pair to come in row 81, last pair to come just below neck shaping, and rem 2 pairs evenly spaced between.

RIGHT FRONT
Using 6mm (US 10) needles cast on 57 [61: 65: 69] sts.
Work in g st, dec 1 st at end of 11th and every foll 10th row until 50 [54: 58: 62] sts rem.
Work 9 rows, ending with RS facing for next row.
Row 81 (RS): K3, cast off 2 sts (to make a buttonhole – cast on 2 sts over these cast-off sts on next row), K until there are 13 sts on right needle after cast-off, cast off 2 sts (to make 2nd buttonhole of this pair), K to last 2 sts, K2tog.
Making a further 3 pairs of buttonholes in this way to correspond with positions marked for buttons on left front, complete to match left front, reversing shapings.

SLEEVES
Using 6mm (US 10) needles cast on 39 [41: 43: 43] sts.
Work in g st, shaping sides by inc 1 st at each end of 15th [15th: 15th: 13th] and every foll 16th [16th: 16th: 14th] row to 53 [53: 51: 53] sts, then on every foll - [18th: 18th: 16th] row until there are - [55: 57: 59] sts.
Cont straight until sleeve meas 45 [46: 47: 47] cm, ending with RS facing for next row.
Shape top
Keeping patt correct, cast off 5 sts at beg of next 2 rows. 43 [45: 47: 49] sts.
Dec 1 st at each end of next 3 rows, then on foll alt row, then on every foll 6th row until 27 [29: 31: 33] sts rem.
Work 3 rows, ending with RS facing for next row.
Dec 1 st at each end of next and every foll alt row to 19 sts, then on foll row, ending with RS facing for next row.
Cast off rem 13 sts.

MAKING UP
Press as described on the information page.

Join both shoulder seams using back stitch, or mattress stitch if preferred.

Scarf

Using 6mm (US 10) needles cast on 30 sts.

Work in g st until scarf meas 80 cm, ending with RS facing for next row.

Place marker at end of last row.

Cont in g st until scarf, from marker, fits around neck edge, beg and ending at inner edge of cast-off sts at beg of neck shaping.

Cont in g st for a further 80 cm.

Cast off.

Sew scarf to neck edge, leaving cast-off sts at beg of neck shaping free.

See information page for finishing instructions, setting in sleeves using the set-in method.

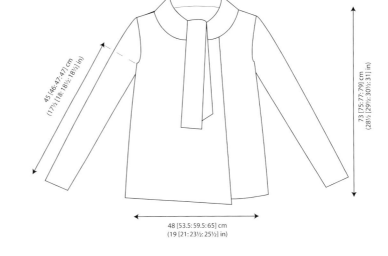

45 [46:46:47:47] cm
(17½ [18:18:18½:18½] in)

73 [75:77:77:79] cm
(28½ [29½:30½:30½:31] in)

48 [53.5:59.5:65] cm
(19 [21:23½:25½] in)

Main image page 36

Douglas

YARN

	S	M	L	XL	XXL	
To fit chest	102	107	112	117	122	cm
	40	42	44	46	48	in

Rowan RYC Cashsoft Aran

| | 24 | 25 | 27 | 28 | 33 | x 50gm |

(photographed in Thunder 014)

NEEDLES

1 pair 4mm (no 8) (US 6) needles
1 pair 4½mm (no 7) (US 7) needles
Cable needle

BUTTONS – 10 x 00335

TENSION

27 sts and 25 rows to 10 cm measured over pattern using 4½mm (US 7) needles.

SPECIAL ABBREVIATIONS

C6B = slip next 3 sts onto cable needle and leave at back of work, K3, then K3 from cable needle;
C6F = slip next 3 sts onto cable needle and leave at front of work, K3, then K3 from cable needle.

BACK

Using 4mm (US 6) needles cast on 150 [158: 166: 174: 182] sts.
Row 1 (RS): P2, *K2, P2, rep from * to end.
Row 2: K2, *P2, K2, rep from * to end.
These 2 rows form rib.
Work in rib for a further 19 rows, ending with **WS** facing for next row.
Row 22 (WS): Rib 41 [45: 49: 53: 57], (M1, rib 4, M1, rib 28) twice, M1, rib 4, M1, rib to end.
156 [164: 172: 180: 188] sts.
Change to 4½mm (US 7) needles.
Cont in rib and cable patt as folls:
Row 1 (RS): Rib 38 [42: 46: 50: 54], (K12, rib 22) twice, K12, rib to end.
Row 2: Rib 38 [42: 46: 50: 54], (P12, rib 22) twice, P12, rib to end.
Rows 3 and 4: As rows 1 and 2.
Row 5: Rib 38 [42: 46: 50: 54], (C6B, C6F, rib 22) twice, C6B, C6F, rib to end.
Row 6: As row 2.
Rows 7 to 10: As rows 1 and 2, twice.
These 10 rows form cable and rib patt.

Cont in patt as set for a further 68 rows, ending with RS facing for next row.
Shape raglan armholes
Keeping patt correct, cast off 3 sts at beg of next 2 rows. 150 [158: 166: 174: 182] sts.
Dec 1 st at each end of next 31 [37: 41: 47: 51] rows, then on every foll alt row until 52 [52: 54: 54: 56] sts rem.
Work 1 row, ending with RS facing for next row.
Cast off.

LEFT FRONT

Using 4mm (US 6) needles cast on 100 [104: 108: 112: 116] sts.
Row 1 (RS): *P2, K2, rep from * to end.
Row 2: As row 1.
These 2 rows form rib.
Work in rib for a further 2 rows, ending with RS facing for next row.
Row 5 (buttonhole row) (RS): Rib 56 [60: 64: 68: 72], cast off 2 sts (to make first buttonhole of first pair – cast on 2 sts over these cast-off sts on next row), rib to last 8 sts, cast off 2 sts (to make 2nd buttonhole of this first pair – cast on 2 sts over these cast-off sts on next row), rib to end.
Work in rib for a further 16 rows, ending with **WS** facing for next row.
Row 22 (WS): Rib 23, M1, rib 4, M1, rib 28, M1, rib 4, M1, rib to end. 104 [108: 112: 116: 120] sts.
Change to 4½mm (US 7) needles.
Cont in rib and cable patt as folls:
Row 1 (RS): Rib 38 [42: 46: 50: 54], K12, rib 22, K12, rib to end.
Row 2: Rib 20, P12, rib 22, P12, rib to end.
Row 3: Rib 38 [42: 46: 50: 54], K12, rib 8, cast off 2 sts (to make first buttonhole of 2nd pair – cast on 2 sts over these cast-off sts on next row), rib until there are 12 sts on right needle after cast-off, K12, rib 10, cast off 2 sts (to make 2nd buttonhole of 2nd pair – cast on 2 sts over these cast-off sts on next row), rib to end.
Row 4: As row 2.
Row 5: Rib 38 [42: 46: 50: 54], C6B, C6F, rib 22, C6B, C6F, rib to end.
Row 6: As row 2.
Rows 7 to 10: As rows 1 and 2, twice.
These 10 rows form cable and rib patt and set buttonholes.

Cont in patt as set for a further 56 rows, making a further 3 pairs of buttonholes in 13th and 2 foll 20th rows and ending with RS facing for next row.
Shape front slope
Keeping patt correct, dec 1 st at end of next row and at same edge on foll 11 rows, ending with RS facing for next row. 92 [96: 100: 104: 108] sts.
Shape raglan armhole
Keeping patt correct, cast off 3 sts at beg and dec 1 st at end of next row. 88 [92: 96: 100: 104] sts.
Dec 1 st at front slope edge of next row. 87 [91: 95: 99: 103] sts.
Dec 1 st at raglan armhole edge of next 31 [37: 41: 47: 51] rows, then on foll 16 [14: 13: 11: 10] alt rows **and at same time** dec 1 st at front slope edge of next 13 [11: 11: 9: 9] rows, then on foll 25 [27: 28: 30: 31] alt rows. 2 sts.
Work 1 row, ending with RS facing for next row.
Next row (RS): K2tog and fasten off.

RIGHT FRONT

Using 4mm (US 6) needles cast on 100 [104: 108: 112: 116] sts.
Row 1 (RS): *K2, P2, rep from * to end.
Row 2: As row 1.
These 2 rows form rib.
Work in rib for a further 19 rows, ending with **WS** facing for next row.
Row 22 (WS): Rib 41 [45: 49: 53: 57], M1, rib 4, M1, rib 28, M1, rib 4, M1, rib to end.
104 [108: 112: 116: 120] sts.
Change to 4½mm (US 7) needles.
Cont in rib and cable patt as folls:
Row 1 (RS): Rib 20, K12, rib 22, K12, rib to end.
Row 2: Rib 38 [42: 46: 50: 54], P12, rib 22, P12, rib to end.
Rows 3 and 4: As rows 1 and 2.
Row 5: Rib 20, C6B, C6F, rib 22, C6B, C6F, rib to end.
Row 6: As row 2.
Rows 7 to 10: As rows 1 and 2, twice.
These 10 rows form cable and rib patt.
Complete to match left front, reversing shapings and omitting buttonholes.

SLEEVES

Using 4mm (US 6) needles cast on 74 [76: 78: 80: 82] sts.

Row 1 (RS): K0 [0: 0: 1: 0], P0 [1: 2: 2: 0], rep from * to last 2 [3: 0: 1: 2] sts, K2 [2: 0: 1: 2], P0 [1: 0: 0: 0].

Row 2: P0 [0: 0: 1: 0], K0 [1: 2: 2: 0], *P2, K2, rep from * to last 2 [3: 0: 1: 2] sts, P2 [2: 0: 1: 2], K0 [1: 0: 0: 0].

These 2 rows form rib.

Work in rib for a further 19 rows, ending with **WS** facing for next row.

Row 22 (WS): Rib 35 [36: 37: 38: 39], M1, rib 4, M1, rib to end. 76 [78: 80: 82: 84] sts.

Change to 4½mm (US 7) needles.

Cont in rib and cable patt as folls:

Row 1 (RS): Rib 32 [33: 34: 35: 36], K12, rib to end.

Row 2: Rib 32 [33: 34: 35: 36], P12, rib to end.

Row 3: (Inc in first st) 1 [1: 1: 0: 0] times, rib 31 [32: 33: 35: 36], K12, rib to last 1 [1: 1: 0: 0] st, (inc in last st) 1 [1: 1: 0: 0] times. 78 [80: 82: 82: 84] sts.

Row 4: Rib 33 [34: 35: 35: 36], P12, rib to end.

Row 5: (Inc in first st) 0 [0: 0: 1: 1] times, rib 33 [34: 35: 34: 35], C6B, C6F, rib to last 0 [0: 0: 1: 1] st, (inc in last st) 0 [0: 0: 1: 1] times. 78 [80: 82: 84: 86] sts.

Row 6: Rib 33 [34: 35: 36: 37], P12, rib to end.

Row 7: (Inc in first st) 1 [1: 0: 0: 0] times, rib 32 [33: 35: 36: 37], K12, rib to last 1 [1: 0: 0: 0] st, (inc in last st) 1 [1: 0: 0: 0] times. 80 [82: 82: 84: 86] sts.

Row 8: Rib 34 [35: 35: 36: 37], P12, rib to end.

Row 9: (Inc in first st) 0 [0: 1: 0: 0] times, rib 34 [35: 34: 36: 37], K12, rib to last 0 [0: 1: 0: 0] st, (inc in last st) 0 [0: 1: 0: 0] times. 80 [82: 84: 84: 86] sts.

Row 10: Rib 34 [35: 36: 36: 37], P12, rib to end.

These 10 rows form cable and rib patt and beg sleeve shaping.

Cont in patt, shaping sides by inc 1 st at each end of next [next: 5th: next: next] and every foll 4th [4th: 6th: 6th: 6th] row to 88 [86: 116: 116: 112] sts, then on every foll 6th [6th: -: 8th: 8th] row until there are 112 [114: -: 118: 120] sts, taking inc sts into rib.

Cont straight until sleeve meas 52 [54: 56: 58: 60] cm, ending with RS facing for next row.

Shape raglan

Keeping patt correct, cast off 3 sts at beg of next 2 rows. 106 [108: 110: 112: 114] sts.

Dec 1 st at each end of next 31 rows, then on every foll alt row until 12 sts rem.

Work 1 row, ending with RS facing for next row.

Left sleeve only

Dec 1 st at each end of next row, then cast off 3 sts at beg of foll row. 7 sts.

Dec 1 st at beg of next row, then cast off 3 sts at beg of foll row.

Right sleeve only

Cast off 4 sts at beg and dec 1 st at end of next row. 7 sts.

Work 1 row.

Cast off 3 sts at beg and dec 1 st at end of next row.

Work 1 row.

Both sleeves

Cast off rem 3 sts.

MAKING UP

Press as described on the information page.

Join all raglan seams using back stitch, or mattress stitch if preferred.

Collar

Using 4mm (US 6) needles cast on 222 [226: 234: 238: 246] sts.

Work in rib as given for back for 2 rows, ending with RS facing for next row.

Keeping rib correct, cast off 3 sts at beg of next 50 [50: 52: 52: 54] rows.

Cast off rem 72 [76: 78: 82: 84] sts.

Sew shaped cast-off edge of collar to neck edge, matching row-end edges of collar to beg of front slope shaping.

See information page for finishing instructions.

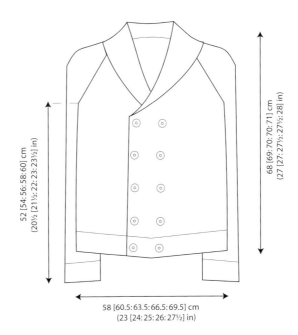

52 [54: 56: 58: 60] cm
(20½ [21½: 22: 23: 23½] in)

68 [69: 70: 70: 71] cm
(27 [27: 27½: 27½: 28] in)

58 [60.5: 63.5: 66.5: 69.5] cm
(23 [24: 25: 26: 27½] in)

Main image page 26

 Erin

YARN

	S	M	L	XL	
To fit bust	81-86	91-97	102-107	112-117	cm
	32-34	36-38	40-42	44-46	in

Rowan RYC Cashsoft Chunky

	14	15	17	19	x 50gm

(photographed in Chalk 702)

NEEDLES
1 pair 6mm (no 4) (US 10) needles

TENSION
15 sts and 20 rows to 10 cm measured over pattern using 6mm (US 10) needles.

BODY (worked in one piece, beg at back hem edge)
Using 6mm (US 10) needles cast on 71 [79: 87: 97] sts.
Row 1 (RS): sl 1, K1, *P1, K1, rep from * to last st, sl 1.
Row 2: Purl.
These 2 rows form patt.
Cont straight until back meas 80 [82: 84: 86] cm, ending with RS facing for next row.
Divide for fronts
Next row (RS): Patt 26 [30: 33: 38] sts and slip these sts onto a holder for right front, cast off next 19 [19: 21: 21] sts, patt to end.
Work on this last set of 26 [30: 33: 38] sts for left front.
Next row (WS): Purl.

Next row: sl 1, patt to last st, sl 1.
These 2 rows set the sts.
Cont as set until work meas 10 cm from cast-off sts, ending with RS facing for next row.
Shape front slope
Next row (RS): sl 1, M1, patt to end.
Working all increases as set by last row, inc 1 st at beg of 4th and every foll 4th row until there are 36 [40: 44: 49] sts, taking inc sts into patt.
Cont straight until left front meas 84 [86: 88: 90] cm from cast-off sts, ending with RS facing for next row.
Cast off.
With **WS** facing, rejoin yarn to rem sts, P to end.
Next row (WS): Purl.
Next row: sl 1, patt to last st, sl 1.
These 2 rows set the sts.
Complete to match left front, reversing shapings.

MAKING UP
Press as described on the information page.
Mark points along outer row-end edges 30 cm from cast-on and cast-off edges. Beg at this point, sew side seams, leaving 23 [24: 25: 26] cm open at upper folded edge for armholes.
See information page for finishing instructions.
Belt
Using 6mm (US 10) needles cast on 9 sts.
Work in patt as given for body until belt meas 150 [160: 170: 180] cm, ending with RS facing for next row.
Cast off.

Cut 35 cm lengths of yarn and, using photograph as a guide, knot groups of 3 of these lengths through every other cast-off and cast-on st of back and front hem edges to form fringe. Make fringe along ends of belt in same way.

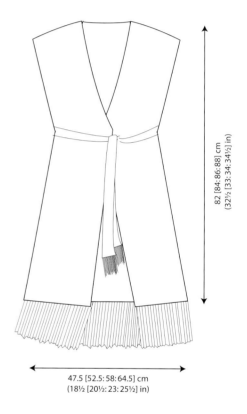

82 [84:86:88] cm
(32½ [33: 34: 34½] in)

47.5 [52.5: 58: 64.5] cm
(18½ [20½: 23: 25½] in)

Main image page 40

 Georgia

YARN

	S	M	L	XL
To fit bust	81-86	91-97	102-107	112-117 cm
	32-34	36-38	40-42	44-46 in

Rowan RYC Cashsoft Aran

	16	18	20	22	x 50gm

(photographed in Oat 001)

NEEDLES

1 pair 4mm (no 8) (US 6) needles
1 pair 4½mm (no 7) (US 7) needles
4mm (no 8) (US 6) circular needle
Cable needle

TENSION

25 sts and 25 rows to 10 cm measured over pattern using 4½mm (US 7) needles.

SPECIAL ABBREVIATIONS

C6B = slip next 3 sts onto cable needle and leave at back of work, K3, then K3 from cable needle;
C6F = slip next 3 sts onto cable needle and leave at front of work, K3, then K3 from cable needle;
C7B = slip next 4 sts onto cable needle and leave at back of work, K1 tbl, P1, K1 tbl, then (P1, K1 tbl) twice from cable needle.

BACK

Using 4mm (US 6) needles cast on 90 [98: 110: 122] sts.
Row 1 (RS): K2, *P2, K2, rep from * to end.
Row 2: P2, *K2, P2, rep from * to end.
These 2 rows form rib.
Cont in rib for a further 25 rows, ending with **WS** facing for next row.
Row 28 (WS): Rib 4 [2: 2: 5], M1, (rib 3, M1) 27 [31: 35: 37] times, rib to end.
118 [130: 146: 160] sts.
Change to 4½mm (US 7) needles.
Row 1 (RS): P0 [0: 0: 1], (K1, P1) 7 [10: 14: 17] times, *P1, (K1 tbl, P1) 4 times, K1, P1, K9, P1, K1, P1, (K1 tbl, P1) 4 times*, K1, P1, K24, P1, K1, rep from * to * once more, (P1, K1) 7 [10: 14: 17] times, P0 [0: 0: 1].
Row 2 and every foll alt row: P0 [0: 0: 1], (K1, P1) 7 [10: 14: 17] times, *K1, (P1 tbl, K1) 4 times, P1,

K1, P9, K1, P1, K1, (P1 tbl, K1) 4 times*, P1, K1, P24, K1, P1, rep from * to * once more, (P1, K1) 7 [10: 14: 17] times, P0 [0: 0: 1].
Row 3: P0 [0: 0: 1], (K1, P1) 7 [10: 14: 17] times, *P1, C7B, P1, K1, P1, C6F, K3, P1, K1, P1, C7B, P1*, K1, P1, (C6B) 4 times, P1, K1, rep from * to * once more, (P1, K1) 7 [10: 14: 17] times, P0 [0: 0: 1].
Row 5: As row 1.
Row 7: P0 [0: 0: 1], (K1, P1) 7 [10: 14: 17] times, *P1, (K1 tbl, P1) 4 times, K1, P1, K3, C6B, P1, K1, P1, (K1 tbl, P1) 4 times*, K1, P1, K3, (C6F) 3 times, K3, P1, K1, rep from * to * once more, (P1, K1) 7 [10: 14: 17] times, P0 [0: 0: 1].
Row 8: As row 2.
These 8 rows form patt.
Cont in patt for a further 26 rows, ending with RS facing for next row.
Keeping patt correct, dec 1 st at each end of next and every foll 12th row until 110 [122: 138: 152] sts rem.
Cont straight until back meas 46 [47: 48: 49] cm, ending with RS facing for next row.**
Inc 1 st at each end of next and every foll 8th row until there are 118 [130: 146: 160] sts, taking inc sts into patt.
Work 7 rows, ending with RS facing for next row.
Shape armholes
Keeping patt correct, cast off 6 sts at beg of next 2 rows. 106 [118: 134: 148] sts.
Cont straight until armhole meas 23 [24: 25: 26] cm, ending with RS facing for next row.
Shape shoulders and back neck
Cast off 10 [12: 15: 17] sts at beg of next 2 rows. 86 [94: 104: 114] sts.
Next row (RS): Cast off 10 [12: 15: 17] sts, patt until there are 15 [17: 18: 21] sts on right needle and turn, leaving rem sts on a holder.
Work each side of neck separately.
Cast off 4 sts at beg of next row.
Cast off rem 11 [13: 14: 17] sts.
With RS facing, rejoin yarn to rem sts, cast off centre 36 [36: 38: 38] sts, patt to end.
Complete to match first side, reversing shapings.

FRONT

Work as given for back to **.

Inc 1 st at each end of next and foll 8th row, taking inc sts into patt. 114 [126: 142: 156] sts.
Work 3 rows, ending with RS facing for next row.
Divide for neck
Next row (RS): Patt 35 [41: 48: 55] sts and turn, leaving rem sts on a holder.
Work each side of neck separately.
Inc 1 st at beg of 4th and foll 8th row, taking inc sts into patt. 37 [43: 50: 57] sts.
Work 7 rows, ending with RS facing for next row.
Shape armhole
Keeping patt correct, cast off 6 sts at beg of next row. 31 [37: 44: 51] sts.
Cont straight until front matches back to beg of shoulder shaping, ending with RS facing for next row.
Shape shoulder
Cast off 10 [12: 15: 17] sts at beg of next and foll alt row.
Work 1 row.
Cast off rem 11 [13: 14: 17] sts.
With RS facing, rejoin yarn to rem sts, cast off centre 44 [44: 46: 46] sts, patt to end.
Complete to match first side, reversing shapings.

MAKING UP

Press as described on the information page.
Join both shoulder seams using back stitch, or mattress stitch if preferred.
Collar
With RS facing and using 4mm (US 6) circular needle, beg and ending at base of front opening, pick up and knit 82 [84: 85: 87] sts up right side of neck, 42 [42: 44: 44] sts from back, then 82 [84: 85: 87] sts down left side of neck. 206 [210: 214: 218] sts.
Beg with row 2, work in rib as given for back for 21 rows, ending with RS facing for next row.
Row 22 (RS): Rib 124 [126: 129: 131], wrap next st (by slipping next st from left needle onto right needle, taking yarn to opposite side of work between needles and then slipping same st back onto left needle) and turn.
Row 23: Rib 42 [42: 44: 44], wrap next st and turn.
Row 24: Rib 56 [56: 58: 58], wrap next st and turn.
Row 25: Rib 70 [70: 72: 72], wrap next st and turn.

Row 26: Rib 84 [84: 86: 86], wrap next st and turn.
Row 27: Rib 98 [98: 100: 100], wrap next st and turn.
Row 28: Rib 112 [112: 114: 114], wrap next st and turn.
Cont in this way, working 14 more sts on every row before wrapping next st and turning, until the foll row has been worked:
Row 33 (WS): Rib 182 [182: 184: 184], wrap next st and turn.
Row 34: Rib to end.
Cont in rib across all sts until row-end edge of collar fits along cast-off edge at base of front opening.
Cast off in rib.
Sew row-end edge of right front end of collar to cast-off sts at base of opening, then sew row-end edge of left front end in place on inside.

Armhole borders (both alike)
With RS facing and using 4mm (US 6) needles, pick up and knit 126 [130: 134: 138] sts evenly along row-end edge of armhole.
Beg with row 2, work in rib as given for back for 8 rows, ending with **WS** facing for next row.
Cast off in rib.

Sew row-end edges of armhole borders to armhole cast-off sts.
See information page for finishing instructions.

84 [86: 88: 90] cm
(33 [34: 34½: 35½] in)

47 [52: 58.5: 64] cm
(18½ [20½: 23: 25] in)

Main image page 20

Moffat

YARN

	S	M	L	XL	
To fit bust	81-86	91-97	102-107	112-117	cm
	32-34	36-38	40-42	44-46	in

Rowan RYC Cashsoft Aran

14	15	17	19	x 50gm

(photographed in Siena 015)

NEEDLES

1 pair 4mm (no 8) (US 6) needles
1 pair 4½mm (no 7) (US 7) needles
Cable needle

TENSION

24 sts and 25 rows to 10 cm measured over pattern using 4½mm (US 7) needles.

SPECIAL ABBREVIATIONS

C4B = slip next 2 sts onto cable needle and leave at back of work, K2, then K2 from cable needle;
C4F = slip next 2 sts onto cable needle and leave at front of work, K2, then K2 from cable needle;
Cr5R = slip next st onto cable needle and leave at back of work, K4, then P1 from cable needle;
Cr5L = slip next 4 sts onto cable needle and leave at front of work, P1, then K4 from cable needle;
C8B = slip next 4 sts onto cable needle and leave at back of work, K4, then K4 from cable needle.

BACK

Using 4mm (US 10) needles cast on 88 [100: 114: 128] sts.
Row 1 (RS): P0 [1: 0: 0], K1 [2: 2: 1], *P2, K2, rep from * to last 3 [1: 0: 3] sts, P2 [1: 0: 2], K1 [0: 0: 1].
Row 2: K0 [1: 0: 0], P1 [2: 2: 1], *K2, P2, rep from * to last 3 [1: 0: 3] sts, K2 [1: 0: 2], P1 [0: 0: 1].
These 2 rows form rib.
Work in rib for a further 19 rows, ending with **WS** facing for next row.
Row 22 (WS): Rib 22 [28: 35: 42], (M1, rib 2) 8 times, M1, rib 4, M1, rib 1, M1, rib 2, M1, rib 1, M1, rib 4, M1, (rib 2, M1) 8 times, rib to end.
110 [122: 136: 150] sts.
Change to 4½mm (US 7) needles.
Cont in cable patt as folls:
Row 1 (RS): K1 [1: 0: 1], (P1, K1) 10 [13: 17: 20] times, work next 28 sts as row 1 of cable panel, P2, K8, P2, work next 28 sts as row 1 of cable

panel, (K1, P1) 10 [13: 17: 20] times, K1 [1: 0: 1].
Row 2: K1 [1: 0: 1], (P1, K1) 10 [13: 17: 20] times, work next 28 sts as row 2 of cable panel, K2, P8, K2, work next 28 sts as row 2 of cable panel, (K1, P1) 10 [13: 17: 20] times, K1 [1: 0: 1].
Row 3: K1 [1: 0: 1], (P1, K1) 10 [13: 17: 20] times, work next 28 sts as row 3 of cable panel, P2, C4F, C4B, P2, work next 28 sts as row 3 of cable panel, (K1, P1) 10 [13: 17: 20] times, K1 [1: 0: 1].
Row 4: K1 [1: 0: 1], (P1, K1) 10 [13: 17: 20] times, work next 28 sts as row 4 of cable panel, K2, P8, K2, work next 28 sts as row 4 of cable panel, (K1, P1) 10 [13: 17: 20] times, K1 [1: 0: 1].
These 4 rows set the sts – 2 cable panels with moss st at sides and cable at centre.
Cont as set until back meas 38 [39: 40: 41] cm, ending with RS facing for next row.
Shape armholes
Keeping patt correct, cast off 6 [7: 8: 9] sts at beg of next 2 rows. 98 [108: 120: 132] sts.**
Dec 1 st at each end of next 3 [5: 7: 9] rows, then on foll 3 [4: 4: 4] alt rows, then on foll 4th row.
84 [88: 96: 104] sts.
Cont straight until armhole meas 20 [21: 22: 23] cm, ending with RS facing for next row.
Shape shoulders and back neck
Cast off 8 [8: 9: 11] sts at beg of next 2 rows.
68 [72: 78: 82] sts.
Next row (RS): Cast off 8 [8: 9: 11] sts, patt until there are 11 [13: 14: 14] sts on right needle and turn, leaving rem sts on a holder.
Work each side of neck separately.
Cast off 4 sts at beg of next row.
Cast off rem 7 [9: 10: 10] sts.
With RS facing, rejoin yarn to rem sts, cast off centre 30 [30: 32: 32] sts, patt to end.
Complete to match first side, reversing shapings.

FRONT

Work as given for back to **.
Dec 1 st at each end of next 3 [5: 7: 9] rows, then on foll 3 [4: 4: 4] alt rows. 86 [90: 98: 106] sts.
Work 3 [1: 1: 1] rows, ending with RS facing for next row.
Divide for front opening
Next row (RS): (Work 2 tog) 1 [0: 0: 0] times, patt 37 [41: 45: 49] sts and turn, leaving rem sts on a holder. 38 [41: 45: 49] sts.

Work each side of neck separately.
Dec 0 [1: 1: 1] st at armhole edge of 2nd row.
38 [40: 44: 48] sts.
Cont straight until 15 [15: 17: 17] rows less have been worked than on back to beg of shoulder shaping, ending with WS facing for next row.
Shape neck
Keeping patt correct, cast off 6 sts at beg of next row. 32 [34: 38: 42] sts.
Dec 1 st at neck edge of next 6 rows, then on foll 2 [2: 3: 3] alt rows, then on foll 4th row, ending with RS facing for next row. 23 [25: 28: 32] sts.
Shape shoulder
Cast off 8 [8: 9: 11] sts at beg of next and foll alt row.
Work 1 row.
Cast off rem 7 [9: 10: 10] sts.
With RS facing, slip centre 8 sts onto a holder, rejoin yarn to rem sts, patt to last 2 [0: 0: 0] sts, (work 2 tog) 1 [0: 0: 0] times.
Complete to match first side, reversing shapings.

SLEEVES

Using 4mm (US 10) needles cast on 44 [46: 48: 48] sts.

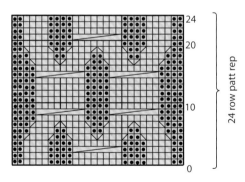

24 row patt rep

Key

□	RS, K WS, P	▣	RS, P WS, K

Cr5R

Cr5L

 C8B

Row 1 (RS): P0 [0: 1: 1], K1 [2: 2: 2], *P2, K2, rep from * to last 3 [0: 1: 1] sts, P2 [0: 1: 1], K1 [0: 0: 0].

Row 2: K0 [0: 1: 1], P1 [2: 2: 2], *K2, P2, rep from * to last 3 [0: 1: 1] sts, K2 [0: 1: 1], P1 [0: 0: 0].

These 2 rows form rib.

Work in rib for a further 19 rows, ending with **WS** facing for next row.

Row 22 (WS): Rib 14 [15: 16: 16], (M1, rib 2) 8 times, M1, rib to last st, inc in last st. 54 [56: 58: 58] sts.

Change to 4½mm (US 7) needles.

Cont in cable patt as folls:

Row 1 (RS): K1 [0: 1: 1], (P1, K1) 6 [7: 7: 7] times, work next 28 sts as row 1 of cable panel, (K1, P1) 6 [7: 7: 7] times, K1 [0: 1: 1].

Row 2: K1 [0: 1: 1], (P1, K1) 6 [7: 7: 7] times, work next 28 sts as row 2 of cable panel, (K1, P1) 6 [7: 7: 7] times, K1 [0: 1: 1].

These 2 rows set the sts – central cable panel with moss st at sides.

Cont as set, shaping sides by inc 1 st at each end of 5th [5th: 3rd: 3rd] and every foll 8th [8th: 6th: 6th] row to 66 [76: 62: 78] sts, then on every foll 10th [-: 8th: 8th] row until there are 72 [-: 80: 84] sts, taking inc sts into moss st.

Cont straight until sleeve meas 45 [46: 47: 47] cm, ending with RS facing for next row.

Shape top

Keeping patt correct, cast off 6 [7: 8: 9] sts at beg of next 2 rows. 60 [62: 64: 66] sts.

Dec 1 st at each end of next 3 rows, then on foll 3 alt rows, then on every foll 4th row until 40 [42: 44: 46] sts rem.

Work 1 row, ending with RS facing for next row.

Dec 1 st at each end of next and every foll alt row to 34 sts, then on foll 5 rows, ending with RS facing for next row.

Cast off rem 24 sts.

MAKING UP

Press as described on the information page.

Join both shoulder seams using back stitch, or mattress stitch if preferred.

Collar

With RS facing and using 4mm (US 6) needles, beg and ending at front opening edges, pick up and knit 28 [28: 30: 30] sts up right side of neck, 31 [31: 33: 33] sts from back, then 28 [28: 30: 30] sts down left side of neck. 87 [87: 93: 93] sts.

Row 1 (RS of collar, WS of body): K1, *P1, K1, rep from * to end.

Row 2: As row 1.

These 2 rows form moss st.

Cont in moss st until collar meas 13 cm from pick-up row, ending with RS of collar facing for next row.

Cast off in moss st.

Right front band

Slip 8 sts left on holder at base of front opening onto 4mm (US 6) needles and rejoin yarn with RS facing.

Row 1 (RS): (K1, P1) twice, inc in next st, K1, P1, K1. 9 sts.

Row 2: (P1, K1) 4 times, P1.

Row 3: (K1, P1) 4 times, K1.

Rep rows 2 and 3 until band, when slightly stretched, fits up front opening edge and along end of collar to cast-off edge, ending with RS of collar facing for next row.

Cast off in rib.

Left front band

Using 4mm (US 10) needles cast on 9 sts.

Beg with row 2, complete as given for right front band.

Slip stitch bands in place, sewing cast-on edge of left front band in place behind pick-up row of right front band.

See information page for finishing instructions, setting in sleeves using the set-in method.

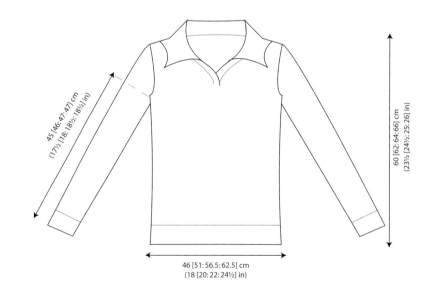

45 [46: 47: 47] cm
(17½ [18: 18½: 18½] in)

60 [62: 64: 66] cm
(23½ [24½: 25: 26] in)

46 [51: 56.5: 62.5] cm
(18 [20: 22: 24½] in)

Main image page 34

Morgan

YARN

	S	M	L	XL
To fit bust	81-86	91-97	102-107	112-117 cm
	32-34	36-38	40-42	44-46 in

Rowan RYC Cashsoft Chunky

| 18 | 21 | 24 | 26 | x 50gm |

(photographed in Blush 703)

NEEDLES

1 pair 6mm (no 4) (US 10) needles

TENSION

15 sts and 20 rows to 10 cm measured over stocking stitch using 6mm (US 10) needles.

BACK

Using 6mm (US 10) needles cast on 70 [78: 86: 96] sts.
Work in g st for 6 rows.
Beg with a K row, work in st st for 14 rows, ending with RS facing for next row.
These 20 rows form patt.
Cont in patt until back meas 34 [35: 36: 37] cm, ending with RS facing for next row.

Shape for sleeves
Keeping patt correct, inc 1 st at each end of next and foll 2 alt rows, then on foll 2 rows, ending with **WS** facing for next row. 80 [88: 96: 106] sts.
Cast on 6 sts at beg of next 4 rows, then 10 [11: 12: 12] sts at beg of foll 2 rows, ending with **WS** facing for next row. 124 [134: 144: 154] sts.
Next row (WS): K12, patt to last 12 sts, K12.
This row sets the sts – first and last 12 sts now worked in g st with all other sts still in patt.
Cont as set until back meas 25 [26: 27: 28] cm from last set of cast-on sts, ending with RS facing for next row.

Shape shoulders and back neck
Cast off 16 [18: 19: 21] sts at beg of next 2 rows. 92 [98: 106: 112] sts.
Next row (RS): Cast off 16 [18: 19: 21] sts, K until there are 20 [21: 23: 24] sts on right needle and turn, leaving rem sts on a holder.
Work each side of neck separately.

Cast off 4 sts at beg of next row.
Cast off rem 16 [17: 19: 20] sts.
With RS facing, rejoin yarn to rem sts, cast off centre 20 [20: 22: 22] sts, K to end.
Complete to match first side, reversing shapings.

FRONT

Work as given for back until 2 rows less have been worked than on back to beg of sleeve shaping, ending with RS facing for next row.

Divide for front opening
Next row (RS): K35 [39: 43: 48] and turn, leaving rem sts on a holder.
Work each side of neck separately.
Next row (WS): K16, patt to end.
This row sets the sts – front opening edge 16 sts now worked in g st with all other sts still in patt.

Shape for sleeves
Keeping sts correct as now set, inc 1 st at beg of next and foll 2 alt rows, then at same edge on foll 2 rows, ending with **WS** facing for next row.
40 [44: 48: 53] sts.
Work 1 row.
Cast on 6 sts at beg of next and foll alt row, then 10 [11: 12: 12] sts at beg of foll alt row, ending with **WS** facing for next row. 62 [67: 72: 77] sts.
Next row (WS): K16, patt to last 12 sts, K12.
This row sets the sts – sleeve edge 12 sts now worked in g st with all other sts as set.
Cont as set until 11 [11: 13: 13] rows less have been worked than on back to beg of shoulder shaping, ending with **WS** facing for next row.

Shape neck
Keeping sts correct as set, cast off 7 sts at beg of next row. 55 [60: 65: 70] sts.
Dec 1 st at neck edge of next 5 rows, then on foll 2 [2: 3: 3] alt rows. 48 [53: 57: 62] sts.
Work 1 row, ending with RS facing for next row.

Shape shoulder
Cast off 16 [18: 19: 21] sts at beg of next and foll alt row.
Work 1 row.
Cast off rem 16 [17: 19: 20] sts.
With RS facing, rejoin yarn to rem sts, K to end.

Next row (WS): Patt to last 16 sts, K16.
This row sets the sts – front opening edge 16 sts now worked in g st with all other sts still in patt.
Complete to match first side, reversing shapings.

MAKING UP

Press as described on the information page.
Join both shoulder seams using back stitch, or mattress stitch if preferred.

Collar
With RS facing and using 6mm (US 10) needles, beg and ending at front opening edges, pick up and knit 24 [24: 26: 26] sts up right side of neck, 28 [28: 30: 30] sts from back, then 24 [24: 26: 26] sts down left side of neck.
76 [76: 82: 82] sts.
Cont in g st until collar meas 13 cm from pick-up row, ending with RS facing for next row.
Cast off.
See information page for finishing instructions.

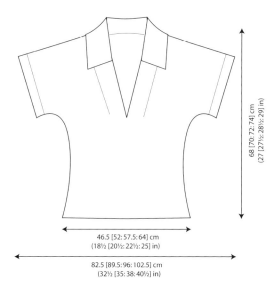

46.5 [52: 57.5: 64] cm
(18½ [20½: 22½: 25] in)

82.5 [89.5: 96: 102.5] cm
(32½ [35: 38: 40½] in)

68 [70: 72: 74] cm
(27 [27½: 28½: 29] in)

Main image page 32

Muir

YARN

	S	M	L	XL
To fit bust	81-86	91-97	102-107	112-117 cm
	32-34	36-38	40-42	44-46 in

Rowan RYC Cashsoft Chunky

| | 18 | 21 | 22 | 23 | x 50gm |

(photographed in Cream 701)

NEEDLES

1 pair 5mm (no 6) (US 8) needles
1 pair 6mm (no 4) (US 10) needles
Cable needle

BUTTONS – 5 x 00421

TENSION

15 sts and 20 rows to 10 cm measured over stocking stitch using 6mm (US 10) needles.

SPECIAL ABBREVIATIONS

C7B = slip next 3 sts onto cable needle and leave at back of work, K4, then K3 from cable needle;
C7F = slip next 4 sts onto cable needle and leave at front of work, K3, then K4 from cable needle.

BACK

Using 5mm (US 8) needles cast on 199 [207: 215: 227] sts.
Row 1 (RS): K17 [18: 19: 19], P3 (mark first of these 3 P sts), *K3, P3, rep from * to last 17 [18: 19: 19] sts (mark last P st), K17 [18: 19: 19].
Row 2: P17 [18: 19: 19], K3, *P3, K3, rep from * to last 17 [18: 19: 19] sts, P17 [18: 19: 19].
Rep last 2 rows 4 times more, ending with RS facing for next row.
Change to 6mm (US 10) needles.
Counting in from both ends of last row, place marker on 48th [50th: 51st: 54th] st from both ends of row, and on centre st – 3 markers in total.
Cont in patt, shaping body as folls:
Row 1 (RS): K to within 2 sts of first marked st, K2tog tbl, K marked st, K2tog, K to within 8 sts of centre marked st, P1, K7, P marked st, K7, P1, K to within 2 sts of last marked st, K2tog tbl, K marked st, K2tog, K to end.
Row 2: P to within 8 sts of centre marked st, K1, P7, K centre marked st, P7, K1, P to end.
Rows 3 and 4: As rows 1 and 2.

Row 5: K to within 2 sts of first marked st, K2tog tbl, K marked st, K2tog, K to within 8 sts of centre marked st, P1, C7B, P marked st, C7F, P1, K to within 2 sts of last marked st, K2tog tbl, K marked st, K2tog, K to end.
Row 6: As row 2.
Rows 7 to 12: As rows 1 and 2, 3 times.
175 [183: 191: 203] sts.
These 12 rows set decreases either side of side markers and form cable patt over centre 17 sts.
Keeping patt correct, dec 1 st each side of side markers (4 sts in total on each dec row) on next and foll 25 [27: 27: 31] alt rows, then on 10 [10: 11: 10] foll 4th rows. 31 [31: 35: 35] sts.
Work 1 row, ending with RS facing for next row.
Cast off.

LEFT FRONT

Using 5mm (US 8) needles cast on 100 [104: 108: 114] sts.
Row 1 (RS): K17 [18: 19: 19], P3 (mark first of these 3 P sts), *K3, P3, rep from * to last 2 [5: 2: 2] sts, K2 [5: 2: 2].
Row 2: P2 [5: 2: 2], K3, *P3, K3, rep from * to last 17 [18: 19: 19] sts, P17 [18: 19: 19].
Rep last 2 rows 4 times more, ending with RS facing for next row.
Change to 6mm (US 10) needles.
Counting in from end of last row, place marker on 48th [50th: 51st: 54th] st from end of row.
Cont in patt, shaping body as folls:
Row 1 (RS): K to within 2 sts of marked st, K2tog tbl, K marked st, K2tog, K to last 9 sts, P1, K7, P1.
Row 2: K1, P7, K1, P to end.
Rows 3 and 4: As rows 1 and 2.
Row 5: K to within 2 sts of marked st, K2tog tbl, K marked st, K2tog, K to last 9 sts, P1, C7B, P1.
Row 6: As row 2.
Rows 7 to 12: As rows 1 and 2, 3 times.
88 [92: 96: 102] sts.
These 12 rows set decreases either side of marker and form cable patt over centre front 9 sts.
Keeping patt correct, dec 1 st each side of marker (2 sts in total on each dec row) on next and foll 25 [27: 27: 31] alt rows, then on 10 [10: 11: 10] foll 4th rows. 16 [16: 18: 18] sts.
Work 1 row, ending with RS facing for next row.
Cast off.

RIGHT FRONT

Using 5mm (US 8) needles cast on 100 [104: 108: 114] sts.
Row 1 (RS): K2 [5: 2: 2], P3, *K3, P3, rep from * to last 17 [18: 19: 19] sts (mark last P st), K17 [18: 19: 19].
Row 2: P17 [18: 19: 19], K3, *P3, K3, rep from * to last 2 [5: 2: 2] sts, P2 [5: 2: 2].
Rep last 2 rows 4 times more, ending with RS facing for next row.
Change to 6mm (US 10) needles.
Counting in from beg of last row, place marker on 48th [50th: 51st: 54th] st from beg of row.
Cont in patt, shaping body as folls:
Row 1 (RS): P1, K7, P1, K to within 2 sts of last marked st, K2tog tbl, K marked st, K2tog, K to end.
Row 2: P to last 9 sts, K1, P7, K1.
Rows 3 and 4: As rows 1 and 2.
Row 5: P1, C7F, P1, K to within 2 sts of last marked st, K2tog tbl, K marked st, K2tog, K to end.
Row 6: As row 2.
Rows 7 to 12: As rows 1 and 2, 3 times.
88 [92: 96: 102] sts.
These 12 rows set decreases either side of marker and form cable patt over centre front 9 sts.
Complete to match left front, reversing shapings.

MAKING UP

Press as described on the information page.
Join both shoulder and overarm seams using back stitch, or mattress stitch if preferred.
Button band
With RS facing and using 5mm (US 8) needles, pick up and knit 119 [119: 125: 125] sts evenly down left front opening edge, from cast-off edge to cast-on edge.
Row 1 (WS): K1, P3, *K3, P3, rep from * to last st, K1.
Row 2: K4, *P3, K3, rep from * to last st, K1.
These 2 rows form rib.
Work in rib for a further 6 rows, ending with **WS** facing for next row.
Cast off in rib (on **WS**).
Buttonhole band
Work to match button band, picking up sts up right front opening edge and with the addition of 5 buttonholes worked in row 4 as folls:
Row 4 (buttonhole row) (RS): Rib 21 [21: 23: 23],

*cast off 2 sts (to make a buttonhole – cast on 2 sts over these cast-off sts on next row), rib until there are 21 [21: 22: 22] sts on right needle after cast-off, rep from * 3 times more, cast off 2 sts (to make 5th buttonhole – cast on 2 sts over these cast-off sts on next row), rib to end.

Collar

Using 5mm (US 8) needles cast on 93 [93: 105: 105] sts.

Row 1 (RS): K3, *P3, K3, rep from * to end.
Row 2: P3, *K3, P3, rep from * to end.
These 2 rows form rib.
Cont in rib until collar meas 20 cm, ending with RS facing for next row.
Cast off 7 [7: 8: 8] sts at beg of next 8 rows.
Cast off rem 37 [37: 41: 41] sts in rib.
Positioning row-end edges of collar halfway across top of front bands, sew shaped cast-off edge of collar to neck edge.

Cuffs (both alike)

With RS facing and using 5mm (US 8) needles, pick up and knit 39 [41: 43: 43] sts evenly across cast-on edge between marked sts either side of overarm seam.
Row 1 (WS): Ko [1: 2: 2], P3, *K3, P3, rep from * to last o [1: 2: 2] sts, Ko [1: 2: 2].

Row 2: Po [1: 2: 2], K3, *P3, K3, rep from * to last o [1: 2: 2] sts, Po [1: 2: 2].
These 2 rows form rib.
Cont in rib until cuff meas 15 cm, ending with RS facing for next row.
Cast off in rib.
Join row-end edges of cuffs.
See information page for finishing instructions.

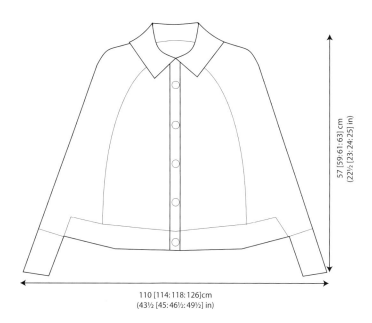

57 [59:61:63] cm
(22½ [23: 24: 25] in)

110 [114:118:126]cm
(43½ [45: 46½: 49½] in)

Main image page 30

 Munro [ladies version]

YARN

	S	M	L	XL
To fit bust	81-86	91-97	102-107	112-117 cm
	32-34	36-38	40-42	44-46 in

Rowan RYC Cashsoft Chunky

| | 20 | 22 | 25 | 27 | x 50gm |

(photographed in Cardinal 709)

NEEDLES

1 pair 5½mm (no 5) (US 9) needles
1 pair 6mm (no 4) (US 10) needles

TENSION

16 sts and 20 rows to 10 cm measured over pattern using 6mm (US 10) needles.

BACK

Using 5½mm (US 9) needles cast on 78 [86: 94: 106] sts.
Row 1 (RS): K2, *P2, K2, rep from * to end.
Row 2: P2, *K2, P2, rep from * to end.
These 2 rows form rib.
Work in rib for a further 14 rows, dec [dec: inc: dec] 1 st at end of last row and ending with RS facing for next row. 77 [85: 95: 105] sts.
Change to 6mm (US 10) needles.
Cont in patt as folls:
Row 1 (RS): P2 [0: 5: 4], K1, *P5, K1, rep from * to last 2 [0: 5: 4] sts, P2 [0: 5: 4].
Row 2: K2 [0: 5: 4], P1, *K5, P1, rep from * to last 2 [0: 5: 4] sts, K2 [0: 5: 4].
These 2 rows form patt.
Cont in patt until back meas 40 [41: 42: 43] cm, ending with RS facing for next row.
Shape raglan armholes
Place markers at both ends of last row to denote base of raglan armholes.
Next row (RS): K2, sl 1, K1, psso, patt to last 4 sts, K2tog, K2.
Next row: P2, P2tog, patt to last 4 sts, P2tog tbl, P2.
Working all raglan shaping as set by last 2 rows, dec 1 st at each end of next 7 [13: 19: 27] rows, then on foll 15 [13: 11: 8] alt rows. 29 [29: 31: 31] sts.
Work 1 row, ending with RS facing for next row.
Cast off.

FRONT

Work as given for back until 33 [33: 37: 37] sts

rem in raglan armhole shaping.
Work 1 row, ending with RS facing for next row.
Shape neck
Next row (RS): K2, sl 1, K1, psso, patt 3 [3: 5: 5] sts and turn, leaving rem sts on a holder. 6 [6: 8: 8] sts.
Work each side of neck separately.
Dec 1 st at neck edge of next 1 [1: 3: 3] rows **and at same time** dec 0 [0: 1: 1] st at raglan armhole edge of 0 [0: 2nd: 2nd] row. 5 [5: 4: 4] sts.
Next row (RS): K2, (sl 1, K2tog, psso) 1 [1: 0: 0] times, (sl 1, K1, psso) 0 [0: 1: 1] times. 3 sts.
Next row: P2tog tbl, P1.
Next row: K2tog and fasten off.
With RS facing, rejoin yarn to rem sts, cast off centre 19 sts, patt to last 4 sts, K2tog, K2. 6 [6: 8: 8] sts.
Dec 1 st at neck edge of next 1 [1: 3: 3] rows **and at same time** dec 0 [0: 1: 1] st at raglan armhole edge of 0 [0: 2nd: 2nd] row. 5 [5: 4: 4] sts.
Next row (RS): (K3tog) 1 [1: 0: 0] times, (K2tog) 0 [0: 1: 1] times, K2. 3 sts.
Next row: P1, P2tog.
Next row: K2tog and fasten off.

SLEEVES

Using 5½mm (US 9) needles cast on 38 [38: 42: 42] sts.
Work in rib as given for back for 16 rows, dec [inc: dec: dec] 1 st at end of last row and ending with RS facing for next row. 37 [39: 41: 41] sts.
Change to 6mm (US 10) needles.
Cont in patt as folls:
Row 1 (RS): P0 [1: 2: 2], K1, *P5, K1, rep from * to last 0 [1: 2: 2] sts, P0 [1: 2: 2].
Row 2: K0 [1: 2: 2], P1, *K5, P1, rep from * to last 0 [1: 2: 2] sts, K0 [1: 2: 2].
These 2 rows form patt.
Cont in patt, shaping sides by inc 1 st at each end of next and every foll 4th row to 51 [51: 51: 57] sts, then on every foll 6th row until there are 63 [65: 67: 69] sts, taking inc sts into patt.
Cont straight until sleeve meas 45 [46: 47: 47] cm, ending with RS facing for next row.
Shape raglan
Place markers at both ends of last row to denote base of raglan armholes.
Working all decreases as set by back and front raglans, dec 1 st at each end of next 11 rows, then

on every foll alt row until 13 sts rem.
Work 1 row, ending with RS facing for next row.
Cast off.

MAKING UP

Press as described on the information page.
Join both front and right back raglan seams using back stitch, or mattress stitch if preferred.
Collar
With RS facing and using 5½mm (US 9) needles, pick up and knit 13 sts from left sleeve, 3 [3: 6: 6] sts down left side of neck, 19 sts from front, 3 [3: 6: 6] sts up right side of neck, 13 sts from right sleeve, then 27 [27: 29: 29] sts from back. 78 [78: 86: 86] sts.
Beg with row 1, work in rib as given for back until collar meas 8 cm from pick-up row.
Change to 6mm (US 10) needles.
Cont in rib until collar meas 19 cm from pick-up row, ending with RS of collar facing for next row.
Cast off in rib.
See information page for finishing instructions.

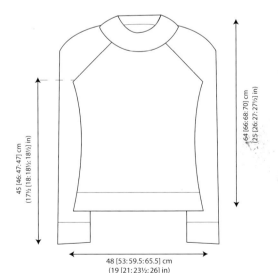

64 [66: 68: 70] cm
(25 [26: 27: 27½] in)

45 [46: 47: 47] cm
(17½ [18: 18½: 18½] in)

48 [53: 59.5: 65.5] cm
(19 [21: 23½: 26] in)

Main image page 18

 Munro [mens version]

YARN

	S	M	L	XL	XXL	
To fit chest	102	107	112	117	122	cm
	40	42	44	46	48	in

Rowan RYC Cashsoft Chunky

| | 23 | 25 | 27 | 29 | 30 | x 50gm |

(photographed in Thunder 708)

NEEDLES

1 pair 5½mm (no 5) (US 9) needles
1 pair 6mm (no 4) (US 10) needles

TENSION

16 sts and 20 rows to 10 cm measured over pattern using 6mm (US 10) needles.

BACK

Using 5½mm (US 9) needles cast on 94 [98: 102: 106: 114] sts.
Row 1 (RS): K2, *P2, K2, rep from * to end.
Row 2: P2, *K2, P2, rep from * to end.
These 2 rows form rib.
Work in rib for a further 14 rows, dec [dec: inc: inc: dec] 1 st at end of last row and ending with RS facing for next row. 93 [97: 103: 107: 113] sts.
Change to 6mm (US 10) needles.
Cont in patt as folls:
Row 1 (RS): P4 [0: 3: 5: 2], K1, *P5, K1, rep from * to last 4 [0: 3: 5: 2] sts, P4 [0: 3: 5: 2].
Row 2: K4 [0: 3: 5: 2], P1, *K5, P1, rep from * to last 4 [0: 3: 5: 2] sts, K4 [0: 3: 5: 2].
These 2 rows form patt.
Cont in patt until back meas 38 [39: 38: 39: 38] cm, ending with RS facing for next row.
Shape raglan armholes
Place markers at both ends of last row to denote base of raglan armholes.
Next row (RS): K2, sl 1, K1, psso, patt to last 4 sts, K2tog, K2.
Next row: P2, P2tog, patt to last 4 sts, P2tog tbl, P2.
Working all raglan shaping as set by last 2 rows, dec 1 st at each end of next 11 [13: 15: 17: 19] rows, then on foll 17 alt rows. 33 [33: 35: 35: 37] sts.
Work 1 row, ending with RS facing for next row.
Cast off.

FRONT

Work as given for back until 37 [37: 41: 41: 45] sts

rem in raglan armhole shaping.
Work 1 row, ending with RS facing for next row.
Shape neck
Next row (RS): K2, sl 1, K1, psso, patt 3 [3: 5: 5: 7] sts and turn, leaving rem sts on a holder. 6 [6: 8: 8: 10] sts.
Work each side of neck separately.
Dec 1 st at neck edge of next 1 [1: 3: 3: 3] rows, then on foll 0 [0: 0: 0: 1] alt row **and at same time** dec 0 [0: 1: 1: 1] st at raglan armhole edge of 0 [0: 2nd: 2nd: 2nd] and foll 0 [0: 0: 0: 1] alt row. 5 [5: 4: 4: 4] sts.
Next row (RS): K2, (sl 1, K2tog, psso) 1 [1: 0: 0: 0] times, (sl 1, K1, psso) 0 [0: 1: 1: 1] times. 3 sts.
Next row: P2tog tbl, P1.
Next row: K2tog and fasten off.
With RS facing, rejoin yarn to rem sts, cast off centre 23 sts, patt to last 4 sts, K2tog, K2. 6 [6: 8: 8: 10] sts.
Dec 1 st at neck edge of next 1 [1: 3: 3: 3] rows, then on foll 0 [0: 0: 0: 1] alt row **and at same time** dec 0 [0: 1: 1: 1] st at raglan armhole edge of 0 [0: 2nd: 2nd: 2nd] and foll 0 [0: 0: 0: 1] alt row. 5 [5: 4: 4: 4] sts.
Next row (RS): (K3tog) 1 [1: 0: 0: 0] times, (K2tog) 0 [0: 1: 1: 1] times, K2. 3 sts.
Next row: P1, P2tog.
Next row: K2tog and fasten off.

SLEEVES

Using 5½mm (US 9) needles cast on 42 [42: 46: 46: 50] sts.
Work in rib as given for back for 16 rows, dec [inc: dec: inc: dec] 1 st at end of last row and ending with RS facing for next row. 41 [43: 45: 47: 49] sts.
Change to 6mm (US 10) needles.
Cont in patt as folls:
Row 1 (RS): P2 [3: 4: 5: 0], K1, *P5, K1, rep from * to last 2 [3: 4: 5: 0] sts, P2 [3: 4: 5: 0].
Row 2: K2 [3: 4: 5: 0], P1, *K5, P1, rep from * to last 2 [3: 4: 5: 0] sts, K2 [3: 4: 5: 0].
These 2 rows form patt.
Cont in patt, shaping sides by inc 1 st at each end of next and every foll 4th row to 59 sts, then on every foll 6th row until there are 73 [75: 77: 79: 81] sts, taking inc sts into patt.
Cont straight until sleeve meas 52 [54: 56: 58: 60] cm, ending with RS facing for next row.

Shape raglan
Place markers at both ends of last row to denote base of raglan armholes.
Working all decreases as set by back and front raglans, dec 1 st at each end of next 9 rows, then on every foll alt row until 17 sts rem.
Work 1 row, ending with RS facing for next row.
Cast off.

MAKING UP

Press as described on the information page.
Join both front and right back raglan seams using back stitch, or mattress stitch if preferred.
Collar
With RS facing and using 5½mm (US 9) needles, pick up and knit 17 sts from left sleeve, 3 [3: 5: 5: 6] sts down left side of neck, 23 sts from front, 3 [3: 5: 5: 6] sts up right side of neck, 17 sts from right sleeve, then 31 [31: 35: 35: 37] sts from back. 94 [94: 102: 102: 106] sts.
Beg with row 1, work in rib as given for back until collar meas 8 cm from pick-up row.
Change to 6mm (US 10) needles.
Cont in rib until collar meas 19 cm from pick-up row, ending with RS of collar facing for next row.
Cast off in rib.
See information page for finishing instructions.

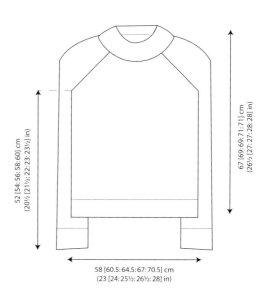

67 [69: 69: 71: 71] cm
(26½ [27: 27: 28: 28] in)

52 [54: 56: 58: 60] cm
(20½ [21½: 22: 23: 23½] in)

58 [60.5: 64.5: 67: 70.5] cm
(23 [24: 25½: 26½: 28] in)

Main image page 16

Paisley

YARN

	S	M	L	XL	
To fit bust	81-86	91-97	102-107	112-117	cm
	32-34	36-38	40-42	44-46	in

Rowan RYC Cashsoft Aran

A Aubergine 017

	18	20	22	24	x 50gm

B Haze 004

	3	4	4	4	x 50gm

C Cream 013

	3	3	3	4	x 50gm

NEEDLES

1 pair 4mm (no 8) (US 6) needles
1 pair 4½mm (no 7) (US 7) needles

BUTTONS – 6 x 00340

TENSION

19 sts and 25 rows to 10 cm measured over stocking stitch using 4½mm (US 7) needles.
21 sts and 22 rows to 10 cm measured over patterned stocking stitch using 4½mm (US 7) needles.

BACK

Using 4mm (US 6) needles and yarn A cast on 99 [109: 119: 131] sts.
Row 1 (RS): K3 [2: 1: 1], *P3, K3, rep from * to last 0 [5: 4: 4] sts, P0 [3: 3: 3], K0 [2: 1: 1].
Row 2: P3 [2: 1: 1], *K3, P3, rep from * to last 0 [5: 4: 4] sts, K0 [3: 3: 3], P0 [2: 1: 1].
These 2 rows form rib.
Cont in rib for a further 10 rows, ending with RS facing for next row.
Change to 4½mm (US 7) needles.
Beg with a K row, work in st st until back meas 58 [59: 60: 61] cm, ending with **WS** facing for next row.
Next row (WS): P4 [5: 7: 7], M1, *P10 [11: 8: 9], M1, rep from * to last 5 [5: 8: 7] sts, P to end. 109 [119: 133: 145] sts.
Beg and ending rows as indicated and using the **fairisle** technique as described on the information page, cont in patt from chart, which is worked entirely in st st beg with a K row, as folls:
Cont straight until chart row 42 has been worked,

ending with RS facing for next row.
Shape raglan armholes
Keeping patt correct, cast off 5 sts at beg of next 2 rows. 99 [109: 123: 135] sts.
Dec 1 st at each end of next 9 [17: 19: 19] rows, then on foll 5 [1: 0: 0] alt rows, ending with **WS** facing for next row. 71 [73: 85: 97] sts.
All 63 rows of chart have now been completed.
Break off contrasts and cont using yarn A **only**.
Next row (WS): P7 [8: 6: 7], P2tog, (P16 [16: 12: 14], P2tog) 3 [3: 5: 5] times, P to end. 67 [69: 79: 91] sts.
Beg with a K row, work in st st, dec 1 st at each end of next 1 [1: 7: 17] rows, then on every foll alt row until 29 [29: 31: 31] sts rem.
Work 1 row, ending with RS facing for next row.
Cast off.

POCKET LININGS (make 2)

Using 4½mm (US 7) needles and yarn A cast on 35 sts.
Beg with a K row, work in st st for 40 rows, ending with RS facing for next row.
Break yarn and leave sts on a holder.

LEFT FRONT

Using 4mm (US 6) needles and yarn A cast on 50 [55: 60: 66] sts.
Row 1 (RS): K3 [2: 1: 1], *P3, K3, rep from * to last 5 sts, P3, K2.
Row 2: P2, *K3, P3, rep from * to last 0 [5: 4: 4] sts, K0 [3: 3: 3], P0 [2: 1: 1].
These 2 rows form rib.
Cont in rib for a further 10 rows, ending with RS facing for next row.
Change to 4½mm (US 7) needles.
Beg with a K row, work in st st until left front meas 46 [47: 48: 49] cm, ending with RS facing for next row.
Place pocket
Next row (RS): K7 [10: 12: 15], slip next 35 sts onto a holder and, in their place, K across 35 sts of first pocket lining, K to end.
Cont straight until left front meas 58 [59: 60: 61] cm, ending with **WS** facing for next row.
Next row (WS): P5 [5: 6: 6], M1, *P10 [11: 8: 9], M1, rep from * to last 5 [6: 6: 6] sts, P to end. 55 [60: 67: 73] sts.

Beg and ending rows as indicated, cont in patt from chart as folls:
Cont straight until chart row 42 has been worked, ending with RS facing for next row.
Shape raglan armhole
Keeping patt correct, cast off 5 sts at beg of next row. 50 [55: 62: 68] sts.
Work 1 row.
Dec 1 st at raglan armhole edge of next 9 [17: 19: 19] rows, then on foll 5 [1: 0: 0] alt rows, ending with **WS** facing for next row. 36 [37: 43: 49] sts.
All 63 rows of chart have now been completed.
Break off contrasts and cont using yarn A **only**.
Next row (WS): P8 [8: 6: 7], P2tog, (P16 [17: 12: 14], P2tog) 1 [1: 2: 2] times, P to end. 34 [35: 40: 46] sts.
Beg with a K row, work in st st, dec 1 st at raglan armhole edge of next 1 [1: 7: 17] rows, then on foll 9 [10: 7: 3] alt rows, ending with **WS** facing for next row. 24 [24: 26: 26] sts.
Shape neck
Cast off 8 sts at beg of next row. 16 [16: 18: 18] sts.
Dec 1 st at neck edge of next 5 rows, then on foll 1 [1: 2: 2] alt rows, then on foll 4th row **and at same time** dec 1 st at raglan armhole edge of next and every foll alt row. 3 sts.
Work 3 rows, dec 1 st at raglan armhole edge of 2nd of these rows and ending with RS facing for next row.
Next row (RS): K2tog and fasten off.

RIGHT FRONT

Using 4mm (US 6) needles and yarn A cast on 50 [55: 60: 66] sts.
Row 1 (RS): K2, *P3, K3, rep from * to last 0 [5: 4: 4] sts, P0 [3: 3: 3], K0 [2: 1: 1].
Row 2: P3 [2: 1: 1], *K3, P3, rep from * to last 5 sts, K3, P2.
These 2 rows form rib.
Cont in rib for a further 10 rows, ending with RS facing for next row.
Change to 4½mm (US 7) needles.
Beg with a K row, work in st st until right front meas 46 [47: 48: 49] cm, ending with RS facing for next row.
Place pocket
Next row (RS): K8 [10: 13: 16], slip next 35 sts

onto a holder and, in their place, K across 35 sts of second pocket lining, K to end.
Complete to match left front, reversing shapings.

SLEEVES
Using 4mm (US 6) needles and yarn A cast on 53 [55: 57: 57] sts.
Row 1 (RS): P1 [2: 3: 3], K3, *P3, K3, rep from * to last 1 [2: 3: 3] sts, P1 [2: 3: 3].
Row 2: K1 [2: 3: 3], P3, *K3, P3, rep from * to last 1 [2: 3: 3] sts, K1 [2: 3: 3].
These 2 rows form rib.
Cont in rib for a further 20 rows, ending with RS facing for next row.

Change to 4½mm (US 7) needles.
Beg with a K row, work in st st, shaping sides by inc 1 st at each end of 5th and every foll 6th row to 67 [69: 69: 71] sts, then on foll – [-: 8th: -] row. 67 [69: 71: 73] sts.
Work 2 [4: 6: 2] rows, ending with **WS** facing for next row.
Next row (WS): P5 [6: 4: 5], M1, (P8 [8: 9: 9], M1) 7 times, P to end. 75 [77: 79: 81] sts.
Beg and ending rows as indicated, cont in patt from chart as folls:
Inc 1 st at each end of 3rd [next: next: 3rd] and 1 [0: 0: 1] foll 6th row, then on every foll 8th row until there are 85 [87: 89: 91] sts, taking inc sts

into patt.
Cont straight until chart row 42 has been worked, ending with RS facing for next row.
Shape top
Keeping patt correct, cast off 5 sts at beg of next 2 rows. 75 [77: 79: 81] sts.
Dec 1 st at each end of next 7 rows, then on foll 6 alt rows, ending with **WS** facing for next row. 49 [51: 53: 55] sts.
All 63 rows of chart have now been completed. Break off contrasts and cont using yarn A **only**.
Next row (WS): P4 [5: 6: 7], P2tog, (P11, P2tog) 3 times, P to end. 45 [47: 49: 51] sts.
Beg with a K row, work in st st, dec 1 st at each

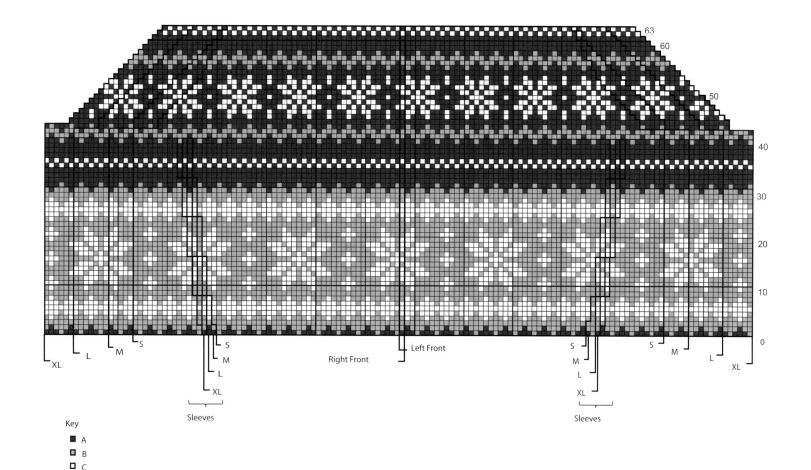

Key
- ■ A
- ▣ B
- □ C

end of next and every foll alt row until 9 sts rem.
Work 1 row, ending with RS facing for next row.

Left sleeve only
Dec 1 st at each end of next row, then cast off
2 sts at beg of foll row. 5 sts.
Dec 1 st at beg of next row, then cast off 2 sts at
beg of foll row.

Right sleeve only
Cast off 3 sts at beg and dec 1 st at end of next
row. 5 sts.
Work 1 row.
Cast off 2 sts at beg and dec 1 st at end of next
row.
Work 1 row.

Both sleeves
Cast off rem 2 sts.

MAKING UP
Press as described on the information page.
Join raglan seams using back stitch, or mattress
stitch if preferred.

Button band
With RS facing, using 4mm (US 6) needles and
yarn A, pick up and knit 257 [263: 263: 269] sts
evenly down left front opening edge, from neck
shaping to cast-on edge.
Row 1 (WS): K1, P3, *K3, P3, rep from * to last st, K1.
Row 2: K4, *P3, K3, rep from * to last st.
These 2 rows form rib.
Cont in rib for a further 10 rows, ending with **WS**
facing for next row.
Cast off in rib (on **WS**).

Buttonhole band
Work to match button band, picking up sts up
right front opening edge and with the addition of
6 buttonholes in row 6 worked as folls:

Row 6 (RS): Rib 101 [102: 102: 103], *cast off 2 sts
(to make a buttonhole – cast on 2 sts over these
cast-off sts on next row), rib until there are
28 [29: 29: 30] sts on right needle after cast-off,
rep from * 4 times more, cast off 2 sts (to make
6th buttonhole), rib to end.

Collar
Using 4mm (US 6) needles and yarn A cast on
95 [95: 101: 101] sts.
Beg with row 2, work in rib as given for button
band for 15 cm, ending with RS facing for next row.
Cast off 7 [7: 8: 8] sts at beg of next 8 rows.

Cast off rem 39 [39: 37: 37] sts.
Sew shaped cast-off edge of collar to neck edge,
placing ends of collar halfway across top of
bands.

Pocket tops (both alike)
Slip 35 sts left on pocket holder onto 4mm (US 6)
needles and rejoin yarn A with RS facing.
Beg with row 2, work in rib as given for button
band for 10 rows, ending with **WS** facing for next
row.
Cast off in rib (on **WS**).
See information page for finishing instructions.

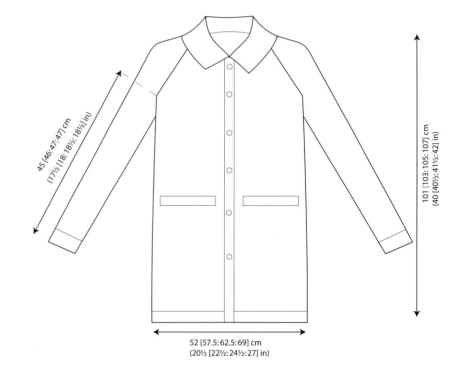

45 [46: 47: 47] cm
(17½ [18: 18½: 18½] in)

101 [103: 105: 107] cm
(40 [40½: 41½: 42] in)

52 [57.5: 62.5: 69] cm
(20½ [22½: 24½: 27] in)

Main image page ?

Paisley hat

YARN

Rowan RYC Cashsoft Aran

A Aubergine	017	2	x 50gm
B Haze	004	1	x 50gm
C Cream	013	1	x 50gm

NEEDLES

1 pair 4mm (no 8) (US 6) needles
1 pair 4½mm (no 7) (US 7) needles

TENSION

21 sts and 22 rows to 10 cm measured over patterned stocking stitch using 4½mm (US 7) needles.

HAT

Using 4mm (US 6) needles and yarn A, cast on 94 sts.
Row 1 (RS): K2, *P2, K2, rep from * to end.
Row 2: P2, *K2, P2, rep from * to end.
These 2 rows form rib.
Work in rib for a further 3 rows, ending with **WS** facing for next row.
Row 6 (WS): Rib 7, M1, (rib 10, M1) 8 times, rib 7. 103 sts.
Change to 4½mm (US 7) needles.

Beg and ending rows as indicated and using the **fairisle** technique as described on the information page, cont in patt from chart, which is worked entirely in st st beg with a K row, until all 23 rows of chart have been completed, ending with **WS** facing for next row.
Break off contrasts and cont using yarn A **only**.
Next row (WS): P5, P2tog, (P8, P2tog) 9 times, P6. 93 sts.
Shape crown
Row 1 (RS): (K5, K2tog) 13 times, K2. 80 sts.
Row 2 and every foll alt row: Purl.
Row 3: Knit.
Row 5: (K4, K2tog) 13 times, K2. 67 sts.
Row 7: Knit.
Row 9: (K3, K2tog) 13 times, K2. 54 sts.
Row 11: Knit.
Row 13: (K2, K2tog) 13 times, K2. 41 sts.
Row 15: (K1, K2tog) 13 times, K2. 28 sts.
Row 16: (P2tog) 14 times.
Break yarn and thread through rem 14 sts. Pull up tight and fasten off securely.

MAKING UP

Press as described on the information page.
Join back seam.

Key

■ A
◨ B
☐ C

Main image page 37

Regan

YARN

	S	M	L	XL	
To fit bust	81-86	91-97	102-107	112-117	cm
	32-34	36-38	40-42	44-46	in
Rowan RYC Cashsoft Aran					
	10	11	12	14	x 50gm

(photographed in Mist 016)

NEEDLES

1 pair 4mm (no 8) (US 6) needles
1 pair 4½mm (no 7) (US 7) needles
Cable needle

BUTTONS – 6 x 00405

TENSION

19 sts and 25 rows to 10 cm measured over stocking stitch using 4½mm (US 7) needles.

SPECIAL ABBREVIATIONS

C6B = slip next 3 sts onto cable needle and leave at back of work, K3, then K3 from cable needle; **C12B** = slip next 6 sts onto cable needle and leave at back of work, K6, then K6 from cable needle; **C12F** = slip next 6 sts onto cable needle and leave at front of work, K6, then K6 from cable needle.

BACK

Using 4mm (US 6) needles cast on 88 [98: 108: 120] sts.
Row 1 (RS): P0 [0: 1: 0], K1 [2: 2: 1], *P2, K2, rep from * to last 3 [0: 1: 3] sts, P2 [0: 1: 2], K1 [0: 0: 1].
Row 2: K0 [0: 1: 0], P1 [2: 2: 1], *K2, P2, rep from * to last 3 [0: 1: 3] sts, K2 [0: 1: 2], P1 [0: 0: 1].
These 2 rows form rib.
Work in rib for a further 19 rows, ending with **WS** facing for next row.
Row 22 (WS): Rib 18 [23: 28: 34], *M1, rib 3, M1, rib 2, M1, rib 3, M1*, rib 36, rep from * to * once more, rib to end. 96 [106: 116: 128] sts.
Change to 4½mm (US 7) needles.
Cont in patt as folls:
Row 1 (RS): Knit.
Row 2: P15 [20: 25: 31], K3, P12, K3, P30, K3, P12, K3, P to end.
Rows 3 and 4: As rows 1 and 2.
Row 5: K18 [23: 28: 34], C12B, K36, C12F, K to end.
Row 6: As row 2.
Rows 7 to 12: As rows 1 and 2, 3 times.
These 12 rows form patt.
Work in patt for a further 2 rows, ending with RS facing for next row.

Divide for belt openings

Next row (RS): K15 [20: 25: 31] and turn, leaving rem sts on a holder.
Next row: Cast on and K 2 sts, P to end.
Next row: Knit.
Next row: K2, P to end.
Rep last 2 rows twice more, ending with RS facing for next row.
Next row (RS): K to last 2 sts, cast off rem 2 sts.
Break yarn and leave these 15 [20: 25: 31] sts on a 2nd holder.
Return to sts on first holder, rejoin yarn with RS facing, patt 18 sts and turn.
Work 8 rows on these 18 sts only, ending with **WS** facing for next row.
Break yarn and leave these 18 sts on a 3rd holder.
Return to sts on first holder, rejoin yarn with RS facing, cast on 2 sts, K30 and turn, leaving rem sts on a holder.
Next row: Cast on and K 2 sts, P to last 2 sts, K2.
Next row: Knit.
Next row: K2, P to last 2 sts, K2.
Rep last 2 rows twice more, ending with RS facing for next row.
Next row (RS): Cast off 2 sts, K to last 2 sts, cast off rem 2 sts.
Break yarn and leave these 30 sts on a 4th holder.
Return to sts on first holder, rejoin yarn with RS facing, patt 18 sts and turn.
Work 8 rows on these 18 sts only, ending with **WS** facing for next row.
Break yarn and leave these 18 sts on a 5th holder.
Return to sts on first holder, rejoin yarn with RS facing, cast on 2 sts, K to end.
Next row: P to last 2 sts, K2.
Next row: Knit.
Next row: P to last 2 sts, K2.
Rep last 2 rows twice more, ending with RS facing for next row.
Next row (RS): Cast off 2 sts, K to end.
15 [20: 25: 31] sts.

Join sections

Next row (WS): P15 [20: 25: 31], patt 18 sts from 5th holder, P30 from 4th holder, patt 18 sts from 3rd holder, then P15 [20: 25: 31] from 2nd holder.
96 [106: 116: 128] sts.
Cont straight until back meas 36 [37: 38: 39] cm, ending with RS facing for next row.

Shape armholes

Keeping patt correct, cast off 6 [7: 8: 9] sts at beg of next 2 rows. 84 [92: 100: 110] sts.
Dec 1 st at each end of next 5 [7: 9: 11] rows, then on foll 3 [3: 2: 2] alt rows, then on foll 4th row.
66 [70: 76: 82] sts.
Cont straight until armhole meas 20 [21: 22: 23] cm, ending with RS facing for next row.

Shape shoulders and back neck

Cast off 6 [7: 7: 8] sts at beg of next 2 rows.
54 [56: 62: 66] sts.
Next row (RS): Cast off 6 [7: 7: 8] sts, patt until there are 10 [10: 12: 13] sts on right needle and turn, leaving rem sts on a holder.
Work each side of neck separately.
Cast off 4 sts at beg of next row.
Cast off rem 6 [6: 8: 9] sts.
With RS facing, rejoin yarn to rem sts, cast off centre 22 [22: 24: 24] sts, patt to end.
Complete to match first side, reversing shapings.

LEFT FRONT

Using 4mm (US 6) needles cast on 44 [49: 54: 60] sts.
Row 1 (RS): P0 [0: 1: 0], K1 [2: 2: 1], *P2, K2, rep from * to last 3 sts, P2, K1.
Row 2: P1, *K2, P2, rep from * to last 3 [0: 1: 3] sts, K2 [0: 1: 2], P1 [0: 0: 1].
These 2 rows form rib.
Work in rib for a further 19 rows, ending with **WS** facing for next row.
Row 22 (WS): Rib 18, M1, rib 3, M1, rib 2, M1, rib 3, M1, rib to end. 48 [53: 58: 64] sts.
Change to 4½mm (US 7) needles.
Cont in patt as folls:
Row 1 (RS): Knit.
Row 2: P15, K3, P12, K3, P to end.
Rows 3 and 4: As rows 1 and 2.
Row 5: K18 [23: 28: 34], C12B, K to end.
Row 6: As row 2.
Rows 7 to 12: As rows 1 and 2, 3 times.
These 12 rows form patt.
Work in patt for a further 2 rows, ending with RS facing for next row.

Divide for belt openings

Next row (RS): K15 [20: 25: 31] and turn, leaving rem sts on a holder.

Next row: Cast on and K 2 sts, P to end.

Next row: Knit.

Next row: K2, P to end.

Rep last 2 rows twice more, ending with RS facing for next row.

Next row (RS): K to last 2 sts, cast off rem 2 sts. Break yarn and leave these 15 [20: 25: 31] sts on a 2nd holder.

Return to sts on first holder, rejoin yarn with RS facing, patt 18 sts and turn.

Work 8 rows on these 18 sts only, ending with **WS** facing for next row.

Break yarn and leave these 18 sts on a 3rd holder. Return to sts on first holder, rejoin yarn with RS facing, cast on 2 sts, K to end.

Next row: P to last 2 sts, K2.

Next row: Knit.

Next row: P to last 2 sts, K2.

Rep last 2 rows twice more, ending with RS facing for next row.

Next row (RS): Cast off 2 sts, K to end.

Join sections

Next row (WS): P15, patt 18 sts from 3rd holder, then P15 [20: 25: 31] from 2nd holder.

48 [53: 58: 64] sts.

Cont straight until left front matches back to beg of armhole shaping, ending with RS facing for next row.

Shape armhole

Keeping patt correct, cast off 6 [7: 8: 9] sts at beg of next row. 42 [46: 50: 55] sts.

Work 1 row.

Dec 1 st at armhole edge of next 5 [7: 9: 11] rows, then on foll 3 [3: 2: 2] alt rows, then on foll 4th row. 33 [35: 38: 41] sts.

Cont straight until 15 [15: 17: 17] rows less have been worked than on back to beg of shoulder shaping, ending with **WS** facing for next row.

Shape neck

Keeping patt correct, cast off 8 sts at beg of next row. 25 [27: 30: 33] sts.

Dec 1 st at neck edge of next 3 rows, then on foll 3 [3: 4: 4] alt rows, then on foll 4th row. 18 [20: 22: 25] sts.

Work 1 row, ending with RS facing for next row.

Shape shoulder

Cast off 6 [7: 7: 8] sts at beg of next and foll alt row.

Work 1 row.

Cast off rem 6 [6: 8: 9] sts.

RIGHT FRONT

Using 4mm (US 6) needles cast on 44 [49: 54: 60] sts.

Row 1 (RS): K1, *P2, K2, rep from * to last 3 [0: 1: 3] sts, P2 [0: 1: 2], K1 [0: 0: 1].

Row 2: K0 [0: 1: 0], P1 [2: 2: 1], *K2, P2, rep from * to last 3 sts, K2, P1.

These 2 rows form rib.

Work in rib for a further 19 rows, ending with **WS** facing for next row.

Row 22 (WS): Rib 18 [23: 28: 34], M1, rib 3, M1, rib 2, M1, rib 3, M1, rib to end. 48 [53: 58: 64] sts.

Change to 4½mm (US 7) needles.

Cont in patt as folls:

Row 1 (RS): Knit.

Row 2: P15 [20: 25: 31], K3, P12, K3, P to end.

Rows 3 and 4: As rows 1 and 2.

Row 5: K18, C12F, K to end.

Row 6: As row 2.

Rows 7 to 12: As rows 1 and 2, 3 times.

These 12 rows form patt.

Work in patt for a further 2 rows, ending with RS facing for next row.

Divide for belt openings

Next row (RS): K15 and turn, leaving rem sts on a holder.

Next row: Cast on and K 2 sts, P to end.

Next row: Knit.

Next row: K2, P to end.

Rep last 2 rows twice more, ending with RS facing for next row.

Next row (RS): K to last 2 sts, cast off rem 2 sts. Break yarn and leave these 15 sts on a 2nd holder.

Return to sts on first holder, rejoin yarn with RS facing, patt 18 sts and turn.

Work 8 rows on these 18 sts only, ending with **WS** facing for next row.

Break yarn and leave these 18 sts on a 3rd holder. Return to sts on first holder, rejoin yarn with RS facing, cast on 2 sts, K to end.

Next row: P to last 2 sts, K2.

Next row: Knit.

Next row: P to last 2 sts, K2.

Rep last 2 rows twice more, ending with RS facing for next row.

Next row (RS): Cast off 2 sts, K to end.

15 [20: 25: 31] sts.

Join sections

Next row (WS): P15 [20: 25: 31], patt 18 sts from 3rd holder, then P15 from 2nd holder.

48 [53: 58: 64] sts.

Complete to match left front, reversing shapings.

MAKING UP

Press as described on the information page.

Join both shoulder seams using back stitch, or mattress stitch if preferred.

Collar

With RS facing and using 4mm (US 6) needles, beg and ending at front opening edges, pick up and knit 28 [28: 31: 31] sts up right side of neck, 30 [30: 32: 32] sts from back, then 28 [28: 31: 31] sts down left side of neck.

86 [86: 94: 94] sts.

Row 1 (WS): K2, *P2, K2, rep from * to end.

Row 2: P2, *K2, P2, rep from * to end.

These 2 rows form rib.

Cont in rib for a further 24 rows, ending with **WS** facing for next row.

Cast off in rib.

Button band

With RS facing and using 4mm (US 6) needles, pick up and knit 116 [120: 124: 128] sts evenly down entire left front opening edge, from top of collar to cast-on edge.

Row 1 (WS): K1, P2, *K2, P2, rep from * to last st, K1.

Row 2: K3, *P2, K2, rep from * to last st, K1.

These 2 rows form rib.

Work in rib for a further 5 rows, ending with RS facing for next row.

Cast off in rib.

Buttonhole band

With RS facing and using 4mm (US 6) needles, pick up and knit 116 [120: 124: 128] sts evenly up entire right front opening edge, from cast-on edge to top of collar.

Work in rib as given for button band for 3 rows, ending with RS facing for next row.

Row 4 (RS): Rib 2 [1: 1: 3], *work 2 tog, yrn (to make a buttonhole), rib 19 [20: 21: 21], rep from * 4 times

more, work 2 tog, yrn (to make 6th buttonhole), rib
to end.
Work in rib for a further 3 rows, ending with RS
facing for next row.
Cast off in rib.

Armhole borders (both alike)
With RS facing and using 4mm (US 6) needles,
pick up and knit 98 [102: 106: 110] sts evenly all
round armhole edge.
Work in rib as given for collar for 5 rows, ending
with RS facing for next row.
Cast off in rib.

Belt
Using 4mm (US 6) needles cast on 12 sts.
Row 1 (RS): Knit.
Row 2: K3, P6, K3.
Row 3: K3, C6B, K3.
Row 4: As row 2.
Rows 5 and 6: As rows 1 and 2.
These 6 rows form patt.
Cont in patt until belt meas 130 [140: 150: 160] cm,
ending with RS facing for next row.
Cast off.

Slip stitch 2 cast-off and 2 cast-on sts in place on
inside at top and bottom of belt openings, then
thread belt through openings as in photograph.
See information page for finishing instructions.

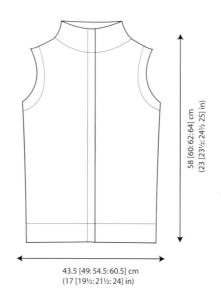

58 [60: 62: 64] cm
(23 [23½: 24½: 25] in)

43.5 [49: 54.5: 60.5] cm
(17 [19½: 21½: 24] in)

Main image page 28

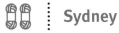

Sydney

YARN

	S	M	L	XL
To fit bust	81-86	91-97	102-107	112-117 cm
	32-34	36-38	40-42	44-46 in

Rowan RYC Cashsoft Aran

	10	11	13	14	x 50gm

(photographed in Forest 018)

NEEDLES
1 pair 4mm (no 8) (US 6) needles
1 pair 4½mm (no 7) (US 7) needles
4mm (no 8) (US 6) circular needle
Cable needle

BUTTONS – 4 x 00410

TENSION
16 sts and 26 rows to 10 cm measured over body pattern using 4½mm (US 7) needles.

SPECIAL ABBREVIATIONS
C4B = slip next 2 sts onto cable needle and leave at back of work, K2, then K2 from cable needle.

BACK
Using 4mm (US 6) needles cast on 66 [74: 82: 94] sts.
Row 1 (RS): K2, *P2, K2, rep from * to end.
Row 2: P2, *K2, P2, rep from * to end.
These 2 rows form rib.

Cont in rib for a further 18 rows, dec [dec: inc: dec] 1 st at end of last row and ending with RS facing for next row. 65 [73: 83: 93] sts.
Change to 4½mm (US 7) needles.
Beg and ending rows as indicated and repeating the 12 row patt rep throughout, cont in patt from chart as folls:
Work 10 rows, ending with RS facing for next row.
Inc 1 st at each end of next and every foll 10th row until there are 73 [81: 91: 101] sts, taking inc sts into patt.
Cont straight until back meas 31 [32: 33: 34] cm, ending with RS facing for next row.
Shape armholes
Keeping patt correct, cast off 3 [4: 5: 6] sts at beg of next 2 rows. 67 [73: 81: 89] sts.
Dec 1 st at each end of next 3 [3: 5: 5] rows, then on foll 1 [2: 2: 4] alt rows. 59 [63: 67: 71] sts.
Cont straight until armhole meas 20 [21: 22: 23] cm, ending with RS facing for next row.
Shape shoulders and back neck
Next row (RS): Cast off 7 [8: 8: 9] sts, patt until there are 10 [11: 12: 13] sts on right needle and turn, leaving rem sts on a holder.
Work each side of neck separately.
Cast off 3 sts at beg of next row.
Cast off rem 7 [8: 9: 10] sts.
With RS facing, rejoin yarn to rem sts, cast off centre 25 [25: 27: 27] sts, patt to end.
Complete to match first side, reversing shapings.

LEFT FRONT
Using 4mm (US 6) needles cast on 30 [34: 38: 42] sts.
Work in rib as given for back for 20 rows, inc 0 [0: 1: 2] sts evenly across last row and ending with RS facing for next row. 30 [34: 39: 44] sts.
Change to 4½mm (US 7) needles.
Beg and ending rows as indicated, cont in patt from chart as folls:
Work 10 rows, ending with RS facing for next row.
Inc 1 st at beg of next and every foll 10th row until there are 34 [38: 43: 48] sts, taking inc sts into patt.
Cont straight until left front matches back to beg of armhole shaping, ending with RS facing for next row.
Shape armhole and front slope
Keeping patt correct, cast off 3 [4: 5: 6] sts at beg and dec 1 st at end of next row. 30 [33: 37: 41] sts.
Work 1 row.
Dec 1 st at armhole edge of next 3 [3: 5: 5] rows, then on foll 1 [2: 2: 4] alt rows **and at same time** dec 1 st at front slope edge on next [next: next: 3rd] and foll 1 [0: 0: 0] alt rows, then on 0 [1: 2: 2] foll 4th rows. 24 [26: 27: 29] sts.
Dec 1 st at front slope edge **only** on 2nd [2nd: 4th: 2nd] and every foll 4th row until 14 [16: 17: 19] sts rem.
Cont straight until left front matches back to beg of shoulder shaping, ending with RS facing for next row.

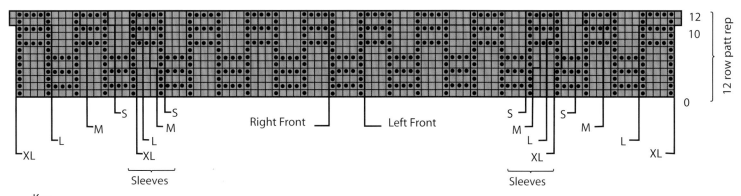

Key

▣ = P on RS, K on WS

▢ = K on RS, P on WS

Shape shoulder
Cast off 7 [8: 8: 9] sts at beg of next row.
Work 1 row.
Cast off rem 7 [8: 9: 10] sts.

RIGHT FRONT
Using 4mm (US 6) needles cast on 30 [34: 38: 42] sts.
Work in rib as given for back for 20 rows, inc 0 [0: 1: 2] sts evenly across last row and ending with RS facing for next row. 30 [34: 39: 44] sts.
Change to 4½mm (US 7) needles.
Beg and ending rows as indicated and repeating the 12 row patt rep throughout, cont in patt from chart as folls:
Work 10 rows, ending with RS facing for next row.
Inc 1 st at end of next and every foll 10th row until there are 34 [38: 43: 48] sts, taking inc sts into patt.
Complete to match left front, reversing shapings.

SLEEVES
Using 4mm (US 6) needles cast on 38 [42: 42: 42] sts.
Work in rib as given for back for 19 rows, ending with **WS** facing for next row.
Row 20 (WS): Rib 1 [5: 3: 3], inc in next st, (rib 1, inc in next st) 17 [15: 17: 17] times, rib 2 [6: 4: 4]. 56 [58: 60: 60] sts.
Change to 4½mm (US 7) needles.
Cont in cable patt as folls:
Row 1 (RS): K0 [1: 2: 2], *P2, K4, rep from * to last 2 [3: 4: 4] sts, P2, K0 [1: 2: 2].
Row 2 and every foll alt: P0 [1: 2: 2], *K2, P4, rep from * to last 2 [3: 4: 4] sts, K2, P0 [1: 2: 2].
Row 3: K0 [1: 2: 2], *P2, C4B, rep from * to last 2 [3: 4: 4] sts, P2, K0 [1: 2: 2].
Row 5: As row 1.
Row 6: As row 2.
These 6 rows form cable patt.
Cont in cable patt, shaping sides by inc 1 st at each end of 3rd [next: next: next] and every foll 10th [8th: 8th: 6th] row to 68 [62: 70: 66] sts, then on every foll – [10th: 10th: 8th] row until there are - [72: 76: 78] sts, taking inc sts into patt.
Work 10 [4: 0: 2] rows, ending with **WS** facing for next row.

Next row (WS): Patt 1 [8: 1: 2] sts, work 2 tog, (patt 2 [1: 2: 2] sts, work 2 tog) 16 [18: 18: 18] times, patt to end. 51 [53: 57: 59] sts.
Beg and ending rows as indicated, cont in patt from chart as folls:
Inc 1 st at each end of 13th [5th: 9th: 5th] and every foll – [10th: 10th: 8th] row until there are 53 [57: 61: 65] sts, taking inc sts into patt.
Cont straight until sleeve meas 45 [46: 47: 47] cm, ending with RS facing for next row.
Shape top
Keeping patt correct, cast off 3 [4: 5: 6] sts at beg of next 2 rows. 47 [49: 51: 53] sts.
Dec 1 st at each end of next 3 rows, then on alt row, then on foll 4th row. 35 [37: 39: 41] sts.
Work 1 row.
Dec 1 st at each end of next and every foll alt row to 23 sts, then on foll 3 rows, ending with RS facing for next row. 17 sts.
Cast off 4 sts at beg of next 2 rows.
Cast off rem 9 sts.

MAKING UP
Press as described on the information page.

Join both shoulder seams using back stitch, or mattress stitch if preferred.
Front border
With RS facing and using 4mm (US 6) circular needle, beg and ending at cast-on edges, pick up and knit 54 [56: 58: 60] sts up right front opening edge to beg of front slope shaping, 38 [40: 42: 44] sts up right front slope to shoulder, 30 [30: 34: 34] sts from back, 38 [40: 42: 44] sts down left front slope to beg of front slope shaping, then 54 [56: 58: 60] sts down left front opening edge. 214 [222: 234: 242] sts.
Beg with row 2, work in rib as given for back for 3 rows, ending with RS facing for next row.
Row 4 (RS): Rib 2 [2: 3: 3], *cast off 2 sts (to make a buttonhole – cast on 2 sts over these cast-off sts on next row), rib until there are 14 [15: 15: 16] sts on right needle after cast-off, rep from * twice more, cast off 2 sts (to make 4th buttonhole), rib to end.
Work in rib for a further 4 rows, ending with **WS** facing for next row.
Cast off in rib (on **WS**).
See information page for finishing instructions, setting in sleeves using the set-in method.

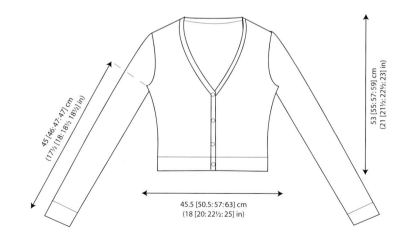

45 [46: 47: 47] cm
(17½ [18: 18½: 18½] in)

53 [55: 57: 59] cm
(21 [21½: 22½: 23] in)

45.5 [50.5: 57: 63] cm
(18 [20: 22½: 25] in)

- Our sizing now conforms to standard clothing sizes. Therefore if you buy a standard size 12 in clothing, then our size 12 or Medium patterns will fit you perfectly.

- Dimensions in the charts below are body measurements, not garment dimensions, therefore please refer to the measuring guide to help you to determine which is the best size for you to knit.

STANDARD SIZING GUIDE FOR WOMEN

UK SIZE	8	10	12	14	16	18	20	22	
USA Size	6	8	10	12	14	16	18	20	
EUR Size	34	36	38	40	42	44	46	48	
To fit bust	32	34	36	38	40	42	44	46	inches
	82	87	92	97	102	107	112	117	cm
To fit waist	24	26	28	30	32	34	36	38	inches
	61	66	71	76	81	86	91	96	cm
To fit hips	34	6	38	40	42	44	46	48	inches
	87	92	97	102	107	112	117	122	cm

CASUAL SIZING GUIDE FOR WOMEN

As there are some designs that are intended to fit more generously, we have introduced our casual sizing guide. The designs that fall into this group can be recognised by the size range: Small, Medium, Large & Xlarge. Each of these sizes cover two sizes from the standard sizing guide, ie. Size S will fit sizes 8/10, size M will fit sizes 12/14 and so on. The sizing within this chart is also based on the larger size within the range, ie. M will be based on size 14.

UK SIZE	S	M	L	XL	
DUAL SIZE	8/10	12/14	16/18	20/22	
To fit bust	32 – 34	36 – 38	40 – 42	44 – 46	inches
	82 – 87	92 - 97	102 – 107	112 – 117	cm
To fit waist	24 – 26	28 – 30	32 – 34	36 – 38	inches
	61 – 66	71 – 76	81 – 86	91 – 96	cm
To fit hips	34 – 36	38 – 40	42 – 44	46 – 48	inches
	87 – 92	97 – 102	107 – 112	117 – 122	cm

STANDARD SIZING GUIDE FOR MEN

UK SIZE	S	M	L	XL	XXL	
EUR Size	50	52	54	56	58	
To fit chest	40	42	44	46	48	inches
	102	107	112	117	122	cm
To fit waist	32	34	36	38	40	inches
	81	86	91	96	101	cm

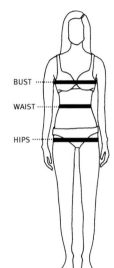

BUST ·····
WAIST ·····
HIPS ·····

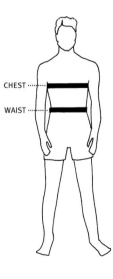

CHEST ·····
WAIST ·····

MEASURING GUIDE

For maximum comfort and to ensure the correct fit when choosing a size to knit, please follow the tips below when checking your size.

Measure yourself close to your body, over your underwear and don't pull the tape measure too tight!

Bust/chest – measure around the fullest part of the bust/chest and across the shoulder blades.

Waist – measure around the natural waistline, just above the hip bone.

Hips – measure around the fullest part of the bottom.

If you don't wish to measure yourself, note the size of a favourite jumper that you like the fit of. Our sizes are now comparable to the clothing sizes from the major high street retailers, so if your favourite jumper is a size Medium or size 12, then our casual size Medium and standard size 12 should be approximately the same fit.

To be extra sure, measure your favourite jumper and then compare these measurements with the size diagram given at the end of the individual instructions.

Finally, once you have decided which size is best for you, please ensure that you achieve the tension required for the design you wish to knit. Remember if your tension is too loose, your garment will be bigger than the pattern size and you may use more yarn. If your tension is too tight, your garment could be smaller than the pattern size and you will have yarn left over. Furthermore if your tension is incorrect, the handle of your fabric will be too stiff or floppy and will not fit properly. It really does make sense to check your tension before starting every project.

stockists

AUSTRALIA
Australian Country Spinners,
314 Albert Street, Brunswick,
Victoria 3056 Tel: (61) 3 9380 3888
Fax: (61) 3 9387 2674
E-mail: sales@auspinners.com.au

AUSTRIA
Coats Harlander GmbH,
Autokaderstrasse 31, A -1210 Wien.
Tel: (01) 27716 – 0 Fax : (01) 27716 - 228

BELGIUM
Coats Benelux, Ring Oost 14A, Ninove,
9400, Belgium Tel 054 318989
E-mail: sales.coatsninove@coats.com

CANADA
Diamond Yarn, 9697 St Laurent,
Montreal, Quebec, H3L 2N1
Tel: (514) 388 6188

Diamond Yarn (Toronto), 155 Martin Ross,
Unit 3, Toronto, Ontario, M3J 2L9
Tel: (416) 736 6111 Fax: (416) 736 6112
E-mail: diamond@diamondyarn.com
www.diamondyarns.com

CHINA
Coats Shanghai Ltd,
No 9 Building , Baosheng Road,
Songjiang Industrial Zone, Shanghai.
Tel: (86- 21) 5774 3733
Fax: (86-21) 5774 3768

DENMARK
Coats Danmark A/S, Nannasgade 28,
2200 Kobenhavn N.
Tel: (45) 35 86 90 50 Fax: (45) 35 82 15 10
E-mail: info@hpgruppen.dk Internet:
www.hpgruppen.dk

FINLAND
Coats Opti Oy, Ketjutie 3, 04220 Kerava
Tel: (358) 9 274 871
Fax: (358) 9 2748 7330
E-mail: coatsopti.sales@coats.com

FRANCE
Coats France / Steiner Frères, 100, avenue
du Général de Gaulle,
18 500 Mehun-Sur-Yèvre.
Tel: (33) 02 48 23 12 30
Fax: (33) 02 48 23 12 40

GERMANY
Coats GMbH, Kaiserstrasse 1,
D-79341 Kenzingen
Tel: (49) 7644 8020 Fax: (49) 7644 802399
www.coatsgmbh.de

HOLLAND
Coats Benelux, Ring Oost 14A, Ninove,
9400, Belgium Tel 0346 35 37 00
E-mail: sales.coatsninove@coats.com

HONG KONG
Coats China Holdings Ltd,
19/F Millennium City 2,
378 Kwun Tong Road, Kwun Tong, Kowloon
Tel: (852) 2798 6886 Fax: (852) 2305 0311

ICELAND
Storkurinn, Laugavegi 59, 101 Reykjavik.
Tel: (354) 551 8258
E-mail: malin@mmedia.is

ITALY
D.L. srl, Via Piave, 24 – 26,
20016 Pero, Milan
Tel: (39) 02 339 10 180
Fax: (39) 02 33914661

JAPAN
Puppy-Jardin Co Ltd,
3-8 11 Kudanminami Chiyodaku,
Hiei Kudan Bldg. 5F, Tokyo
Tel: (81) 3 3222-7076
Fax: (81) 3 3222- 7066
E-mail: info@rowan-jaeger.com

KOREA
Coats Korea Co Ltd, 5F Kuckdong B/D,
935-40 Bangbae- Dong,
Seocho-Gu, Seoul
Tel: (82) 2 521 6262
Fax: (82) 2 521 5181

LEBANON
y.knot, Saifi Village,
Mkhalissiya Street 162, Beirut,
Tel: (961) 1 992211 Fax: (961) 1 315553
E-mail: y.knot@cyberia.net.lb

NEW ZEALAND
Please contact Rowan for details of
stockists

NORWAY
Coats Knappehuset AS, `
Pb 100 Ulset 5873 Bergen
Tel: (47) 55 53 93 00
Fax: (47) 55 53 93 93

SINGAPORE
Golden Dragon Store, 101 Upper Cross
Street #02-51, People's Park Centre,
Singapore 058357
Tel: (65) 6 5358454
Fax : (65) 6 2216278
E-mail: gdscraft@hotmail.com

SOUTH AFRICA
Arthur Bales PTY, PO Box 44644,
Linden 2104
Tel: (27) 11 888 2401 Fax: (27) 11 782 6137

SPAIN
Oyambre, Pau Claris 145, 80009 Barcelona.
Tel: (34) 670 011957
Fax: (34) 93 4872672
E-mail: oyambre@oyambreonline.com

SWITZERLAND
Coats Stroppel AG, CH -5300 Turgi (AG)
Tel: (41) 562981220 Fax: (41) 56 298 12 50

SWEDEN
Coats Expotex AB, Division Craft,
Box 297, 401 24 Goteborg
Tel: (46) 33 720 79 00 Fax: 46 31 47 16 50

TAIWAN
Laiter Wool Knitting Co Ltd, 10-1 313 Lane,
Sec 3, Chung Ching North Road, Taipei,
Tel: (886) 2 2596 0269

U.S.A.
Westminster Fibers Inc, 165 Ledge Street,
Nashua, New Hampshire 03060
Tel: (1 603) 886 5041 / 5043
Fax (1 603) 886 1056
E-mail: rowan@westminsterfibers.com

U.K.
Rowan, Green Lane Mill, Holmfirth,
West Yorkshire, England HD9 2DX
Tel: +44 (0) 1484 681881
Fax: +44 (0) 1484 687920
E-mail: mail@ryclassic.com
Internet: www.ryclassic.com

For all other countries please contact
Rowan for stockist details.